THIS BOOK IS DEDICATED TO THE Stephen G. family, (Author) Stephen G.

THIS BOOK IS DEDICATED TO THE Stephen G.
family, (Author) Stephen G.

Unmasking the Artist: Conquering Imposter Syndrome in Creative Pursuits

Chapter 1: Understanding Imposter Syndrome

Defining Imposter Syndrome

Imposter syndrome represents a complex and multifaceted psychological phenomenon characterized by a persistent and often overwhelming sense of self-doubt, inadequacy, and unease about one's accomplishments and capabilities. This feeling can endure even in the presence of undeniable success, accolades, or external validation from peers, mentors, and society at large. Individuals grappling with imposter syndrome frequently attribute their achievements to factors such as luck, chance, or the assistance of others, demonstrating a troubling tendency to fail to acknowledge their own skills, competence, or the significant hard work they have invested in reaching their goals. This internal conflict can breed a profound and paralyzing fear of being exposed as a "fraud," which significantly undermines one's confidence and enjoyment in both creative pursuits and professional endeavors. Originally introduced in the late 1970s by psychologists Pauline Clance and Suzanne Imes, the concept primarily examined the experiences and challenges faced by high-achieving women, yet it has since expanded into a widely recognized phenomenon that affects individuals across a broad spectrum of demographics, professions, and various creative fields. At the core of imposter syndrome lies a substantial disconnect between how individuals perceive themselves and the reality of their accomplishments and potential. Many artists, writers, and creators wrestle with an internal narrative that continually undermines their achievements and contributions, often leading to a cycle of negative self-talk. They may frequently find themselves comparing their work unfavorably to that of their peers, convinced that others possess intrinsic talent, skill sets, or abilities that they themselves inherently lack. This cognitive distortion creates a vicious cycle; the more they feel like imposters, the more hesitant they become to take necessary risks or pursue new opportunities, further entrenching their feelings of inadequacy and self-doubt. The creative field, which is characterized by subjective evaluations, public scrutiny, and the potential for harsh criticism, can significantly exacerbate these feelings, making it essential to address the underlying causes of imposter syndrome. This effort is crucial in fostering a healthier and more supportive creative environment in which individuals can truly thrive and realize their potential. There are several distinct types of imposter syndrome, each characterized by unique traits, behaviors, and potential repercussions that can significantly affect an individual's life and work experience. The "Perfectionist" sets exceedingly high, often unattainable goals for themselves, leading to intense feelings of failure and frustration when they do not achieve these goals entirely or flawlessly. This perfectionist mindset can create a paralyzing fear of making mistakes, often stifling creativity and innovation. The "Superhero" grapples with an overwhelming and often unrealistic need to excel in every single facet of their life, which can result in burnout, anxiety, and severe stress, ultimately affecting their overall well-being and productivity. The "Natural Genius" tends to equate any struggle with a task or challenge as clear evidence that they are simply not cut out for it, reinforcing a damaging narrative about their abilities and worth. Meanwhile, the "Soloist" believes they must accomplish everything independently, harboring fears that asking for help will expose their perceived inadequacies and weaknesses. Understanding these distinct types can be immensely beneficial for individuals, enabling them to identify their own patterns of thought and behavior more clearly and effectively. This self-awareness paves the way for targeted strategies and interventions aimed at effectively combating imposter syndrome in a meaningful and impactful manner, promoting personal growth and resilience. The impact of imposter syndrome on creativity can be both profound and far-reaching, severely stifling innovation, originality, and the free flow of ideas that are essential in creative endeavors. Individuals may hesitate to share their ideas or concepts due to an overwhelming fear of criticism, rejection, or negative feedback from their peers and audiences. This self-imposed limitation not only hampers personal growth and development but also undermines collaboration and a sense of community within various creative fields. When artists and creators feel insecure about their contributions and talents, they are significantly less likely to engage in constructive dialogues or take creative risks that could lead to exciting new opportunities and breakthroughs. Over time, this disengagement can result in a marked decrease in their involvement with their art and creative pursuits, ultimately diminishing their passion, enthusiasm, and overall satisfaction with their work and artistic endeavors, which can negatively affect their long-term creative journeys. Overcoming imposter syndrome necessitates a multifaceted and comprehensive approach that encompasses self-awareness, cognitive restructuring, and robust support from the community. Recognizing the signs and symptoms of imposter syndrome serves as a crucial first step toward dismantling its hold on one's life and overall well-being. Engaging in reflective practices, such as journaling, mindfulness exercises, or therapeutic interventions, can assist individuals in confronting and effectively challenging their inner critic, fostering a healthier mindset. Additionally, seeking support from peers, mentors, or supportive communities can cultivate a sense of belonging and validation, reminding creatives that they are not isolated in their struggles and experiences. By actively addressing the challenges presented by imposter syndrome, individuals can reclaim their confidence and self-worth, paving the way for authentic self-expression, personal growth, and fulfillment in their creative journeys as well as their professional lives. This process not only enhances their creativity but also enriches their overall life experience.

Historical Context and Origins

The phenomenon of imposter syndrome, characterized by persistent feelings of self-doubt and an overwhelming fear of being discovered as a fraud despite evident success, has roots that extend deep into the fabric of history, influencing countless individuals across various domains. While the specific term "imposter syndrome" was coined in 1978 by psychologists Pauline Clance and Suzanne Imes, the feelings associated with it have been documented and discussed for a much longer period throughout history. Historical figures across diverse fields, including literature, science, and the arts, have often grappled with the internal conflict between their notable achievements and their personal self-perception. The early 20th century, for example, saw many renowned artists and writers, such as Virginia Woolf and Franz Kafka, openly voicing their insecurities and doubts. This highlights that the struggle with self-doubt is not merely a modern invention but rather a longstanding aspect of the creative experience that has persisted through the ages, affecting individuals who have made significant contributions to culture and knowledge. The origins of imposter syndrome can be traced to various societal factors that significantly influence individual identity and self-worth. Cultural expectations, particularly those imposed on artists and creatives, tend to dictate that individuals within these fields must inherently possess an innate talent or genius. This pervasive notion can create immense pressure, compelling artists to constantly measure themselves against an idealized and often unattainable standard. Additionally, the highly competitive nature of creative industries exacerbates feelings of inadequacy and self-doubt, as individuals are frequently compared to their peers and colleagues, fostering an environment rife with tension and anxiety. This historical context reveals that the pressures faced by contemporary creatives are not solely personal struggles but are also shaped by broader societal narratives and expectations that have evolved over time, contributing to the persistent nature of these feelings. In the realm of psychology, the exploration of self-doubt has evolved significantly and rapidly over the decades. Early psychological theories emphasized the role of personality traits in shaping one's self-image and self-assessment. However, as research advanced and expanded, it became increasingly evident that environmental factors, including upbringing, cultural influences, and societal context, play a crucial role in fostering feelings of being an imposter. The recognition of these influential factors has led to a more nuanced understanding of imposter syndrome, particularly in creative pursuits, where the subjective nature of success complicates personal self-assessment. This evolution in thought reflects a significant shift from a purely individualistic perspective to a more holistic view that recognizes and considers the intricate interplay between personal experiences and external influences that shape our sense of self and our understanding of achievement. The impact of historical movements, such as feminism and civil rights, has also significantly contributed to the ongoing conversation surrounding imposter syndrome. These transformative movements challenged traditional notions of identity, success, and achievement, encouraging individuals to redefine their accomplishments in more inclusive and personal terms. As artists and creatives from diverse backgrounds began to share their stories and experiences, the dialogue around self-doubt expanded and became more multifaceted, touching on various dimensions of identity. This shift has paved the way for a more supportive environment where individuals can openly acknowledge their struggles without fear of judgment or ridicule. The growing awareness of imposter syndrome within creative communities has led to a collective effort to normalize these feelings, fostering resilience and solidarity among artists and enabling them to support one another in their creative journeys. Understanding the historical context of imposter syndrome is crucial for contemporary creatives seeking to navigate their own insecurities and challenges in a complex world. By recognizing that these feelings are deeply rooted in societal constructs rather than personal failings or inadequacies, individuals can begin to dismantle the barriers that perpetuate self-doubt and feelings of fraudulence. The journey toward overcoming imposter syndrome is not merely about personal growth and self-improvement; it is also about actively challenging the narratives that have shaped the creative landscape over time. As artists unmask their vulnerabilities and share their personal experiences, they contribute to a cultural shift that increasingly values authenticity over perfection. This, in turn, ultimately empowers themselves and others in their creative pursuits and endeavors, fostering a more inclusive and understanding community that celebrates diverse expressions of talent and creativity.

The Impact of Imposter Syndrome on Creative Professionals

Imposter syndrome is a deeply rooted and pervasive issue that affects a substantial number of creative professionals, frequently manifesting as persistent feelings of self-doubt, inadequacy, and an intense fear of being exposed as a fraud in their respective fields. This psychological phenomenon creates significant barriers to creativity and innovation, compelling individuals to second-guess their abilities and question the validity of their work at every turn. This often leads to a paralyzing sense of uncertainty that can feel overwhelmingly oppressive. The impact of imposter syndrome is particularly pronounced in fields where subjective evaluation and personal expression are essential components, such as art, writing, design, and music. Those grappling with these feelings may find it increasingly challenging to embrace their unique perspectives and inherent talents, leading to a debilitating cycle of anxiety, stagnation, and frustration that can be particularly difficult to break free from. The fear of being unmasked as an imposter can lead to a profound reluctance to share one's work with others, effectively stifling collaboration and the constructive feedback that are vital for growth and development in any creative environment. Creative professionals might shy away from networking opportunities or avoid public presentations entirely, deeply fearing judgment and criticism from peers and critics alike. This isolation can exacerbate feelings of inadequacy, reinforcing the damaging notion that one's achievements are mere luck rather than genuine results of skill, effort, and hard work. Consequently, the very essence of creativity—sharing ideas, engaging in meaningful dialogue, and receiving constructive criticism—becomes compromised, leaving individuals trapped in a persistent cycle of self-doubt and hesitation that can be incredibly hard to break. Moreover, imposter syndrome can severely hinder the creative process itself, creating a significant obstacle to authentic artistic expression. Many individuals may become obsessively perfectionistic, revising and refining their work to the point of total paralysis, unable to move forward with any project or idea. This overwhelming desire for perfection can prevent artists from completing projects or taking necessary risks that are vital for artistic growth, exploration, and self-discovery. The constant comparison to others, fueled by social media and the visibility of peers, further exacerbates this issue. Creative professionals may feel that their work simply does not measure up to the standards set by their colleagues, contributing to a detrimental mindset that stifles originality and experimentation, which are essential components of genuine creativity and groundbreaking innovation. The emotional toll of imposter syndrome can also lead to burnout and diminished job satisfaction over time, creating a negative feedback loop that is profoundly difficult to escape. Creative professionals may experience heightened stress levels, anxiety, and even depression as they struggle with the crippling belief that they are never good enough. This internal struggle can significantly diminish their passion for their craft, leading to a profound disconnection from the very pursuits that once brought them immense joy and fulfillment. Over time, the cumulative effects of these feelings can result in a marked decline in productivity, artistic output, and overall well-being, creating a downward spiral that many find challenging to escape from or even recognize. Addressing imposter syndrome is crucial for the health and long-term success of creative professionals and can lead to transformative changes in their careers and personal lives. Strategies such as cultivating self-compassion, seeking mentorship, and actively reframing negative self-talk can help individuals develop a more positive self-image over time. By acknowledging and confronting these pervasive feelings, creatives can begin to unmask the false narratives that hold them back, allowing for greater authenticity and confidence in their work. Embracing vulnerability, along with understanding that imperfection is an inherent part of the creative journey, can ultimately lead to more fulfilling and innovative artistic endeavors. This, in turn, paves the way for significant growth, exploration, and transformation in their careers and personal lives, enabling them to reclaim their passion and joy in their creative pursuits.

Chapter 2: Recognizing the Signs

Common Symptoms of Imposter Syndrome

Imposter syndrome manifests through a variety of symptoms that can significantly impact an individual's mental health and creative output in numerous ways. One of the most prevalent symptoms is persistent self-doubt, which can become all-consuming and overwhelming, often affecting various aspects of life beyond just creative pursuits. Individuals frequently feel inadequate, deeply convinced that their achievements are merely a result of luck rather than a reflection of their own unique talents or genuine efforts. This nagging doubt can lead artists and creators to constantly question their skills and worth, even when faced with overwhelming evidence showcasing their considerable success. Such feelings can severely hinder their willingness to pursue new opportunities, engage in collaborations with others, or share their work publicly, further isolating them in their struggles and creating a cycle of self-reinforcement in their negative beliefs that can be incredibly difficult to break free from. As a result, individuals may find themselves trapped in a paralyzing loop of self-criticism, where the fear of failure overshadows their potential for growth. Another common symptom is the tendency to downplay accomplishments, which can be remarkably damaging to one's self-image and future prospects. Many individuals grappling with imposter syndrome find it exceptionally difficult to accept praise or recognition, often attributing their achievements to external factors beyond their control, which can lead to a distorted perception of their capabilities. They might frequently say things like, "I was just in the right place at the right time," or "Anyone could have done what I did." This denial of personal merit not only affects self-esteem but can also lead to a reluctance to pursue further development in their craft, as they may feel fundamentally unworthy of any form of growth or advancement. Consequently, this mindset stunts their potential and limits their opportunities for success, creating a self-fulfilling prophecy that reinforces their feelings of inadequacy, making it difficult to envision a path forward that embraces their talents and abilities. Perfectionism is frequently intertwined with imposter syndrome, as those afflicted often set unattainably high standards for themselves that can feel burdensome and overwhelming. This relentless drive for perfection can result in a never-ending cycle of dissatisfaction, where the individual feels that no matter how well they perform, it is simply never good enough in their eyes. This relentless pursuit can stifle creativity in profound ways, as the fear of making mistakes can inhibit essential experimentation and exploration, which are crucial components in any artistic endeavor and absolutely necessary for growth, evolution, and improvement in one's craft. This fear can also lead to avoidance behaviors, where the individual may shy away from taking risks that could lead to new and exciting opportunities, further entrenching their sense of inadequacy and stifling their creative potential. Additionally, many individuals experience profound feelings of isolation and loneliness as they grapple with these emotional challenges. Those suffering from imposter syndrome often believe they are the only ones who feel this way, leading to significant emotional distress and a deep sense of disconnection from others, which can exacerbate their struggles. This pervasive sense of isolation can prevent them from seeking support from peers, mentors, or professional networks, further perpetuating the cycle of self-doubt that binds them. By not sharing their struggles, they miss out on valuable connections, insights, and support that could help them navigate their feelings and foster a sense of community, which is essential for emotional well-being and personal growth. This lack of connection can also contribute to a sense of hopelessness that makes it even more challenging to break free from the confines of imposter syndrome, leaving many to feel as though they are battling their demons in solitude. Lastly, anxiety and stress are common emotional responses linked to imposter syndrome that can manifest in many forms, affecting both mental and physical health in profound ways. The constant pressure to prove oneself can lead to heightened levels of anxiety and stress, which can manifest physically and mentally in various detrimental forms. This chronic stress may ultimately result in burnout, decreased productivity, and a general disconnection from one's creative passion and joy. Recognizing these symptoms is the first and most crucial step in addressing imposter syndrome. By acknowledging their experiences, individuals can seek effective strategies for overcoming these challenges, reclaiming their confidence in their artistic pursuits, and enabling themselves to thrive in their creative endeavors. This journey toward self-acceptance and empowerment can lead to a more fulfilling, enriched, and meaningful life, allowing them to embrace their talents and contributions fully, fostering a sense of belonging and achievement that can help counteract the effects of imposter syndrome.

Differentiating Between Self-Doubt and Imposter Syndrome

Self-doubt and imposter syndrome often intersect in intricate and multifaceted ways, yet they represent distinct psychological experiences that can profoundly impact an individual's creative journey and overall sense of self-worth. Self-doubt refers to a lack of confidence in one's abilities, which leads individuals to question their skills and decisions. In the realm of creative fields, this can manifest as hesitation to share work, an overwhelming fear of criticism, or anxiety about one's innate talent and potential for success. It is a common experience that affects nearly everyone at some point in their lives, stemming from a deep desire for validation and a profound fear of failure. Grasping the nuances of self-doubt is crucial, as it can serve as a significant barrier to expressing creativity and pursuing valuable opportunities that might otherwise enrich one's artistic experiences and personal fulfillment. On the other hand, imposter syndrome is a more pervasive and chronic feeling of inadequacy that persists despite clear and evident success, often leading individuals to feel like frauds in their own achievements. Individuals grappling with imposter syndrome frequently attribute their accomplishments to luck, chance, or external factors rather than recognizing their own abilities, hard work, and dedication. This phenomenon can lead to a persistent and overwhelming fear of being "found out" or exposed as a fraud, which can significantly hinder personal and professional growth. Unlike self-doubt, which may fluctuate based on specific tasks, projects, or situations, imposter syndrome can infiltrate one's identity and self-perception over time, creating a more entrenched sense of inadequacy that can be exceedingly difficult to overcome. Recognizing this critical distinction is essential for effectively addressing the underlying issues and fostering a healthier, more constructive mindset that can promote growth and resilience. To differentiate between the two experiences, consider the specific context in which these feelings arise. Self-doubt may surface during a particular project or presentation, prompting an individual to seek reassurance or constructive feedback from trusted friends, mentors, or peers who can provide valuable insights. In contrast, imposter syndrome can persist across various accomplishments and may even intensify after achieving a significant milestone that one feels unworthy of. For instance, an artist might feel self-doubt while preparing for a gallery show, grappling with whether their work is truly worthy of display in front of a discerning audience. However, if they consistently downplay their success or feel undeserving of accolades and recognition, they are likely experiencing the more chronic and debilitating effects of imposter syndrome, which can erode confidence over time. This awareness can guide individuals toward developing appropriate coping strategies and healthier responses to such feelings, ultimately fostering emotional well-being. Overcoming self-doubt often involves building confidence through consistent practice, self-reflection, and positive reinforcement. Techniques such as setting small, achievable goals, seeking constructive feedback from trusted sources, and celebrating incremental progress can help individuals effectively combat feelings of self-doubt, leading to a more resilient mindset that embraces growth. On the other hand, addressing the complex issues associated with imposter syndrome may require deeper introspection and a reframing of one's beliefs and perceptions about success and failure. Engaging in open discussions with peers, recognizing the commonality of these feelings among creative professionals, and actively challenging negative self-talk can aid in dismantling the false narratives that fuel imposter syndrome, allowing individuals to reclaim their confidence and sense of self-worth. In conclusion, while self-doubt and imposter syndrome share some similarities, they are fundamentally different experiences that require tailored approaches for effective resolution and personal growth. By recognizing the nuanced differences between the two, individuals can better navigate their creative journeys and foster a more fulfilling artistic practice. Embracing vulnerability and seeking support in both instances can lead not only to personal growth but also to a more authentic expression of creativity that resonates deeply with others. Understanding these concepts lays the groundwork for overcoming the barriers they impose, ultimately allowing artists and creatives to thrive and flourish in their pursuits, unlocking their full potential and enriching their lives in profound ways.

Personal Reflection: Identifying Your Triggers

Understanding your triggers is not merely an essential step; it represents a transformative journey in overcoming imposter syndrome, particularly for those who are deeply engaged in the creative arts and face their unique challenges. Triggers encompass the specific thoughts, situations, or interactions that ignite feelings of self-doubt and inadequacy. These triggers often lead to a cycle of negative self-perception that can be challenging to break, creating an emotional landscape that feels constricting and overwhelming. By meticulously identifying these triggers, you can begin to dismantle the ingrained patterns that perpetuate your feelings of being an imposter. This process paves the way for significant and meaningful personal growth and development. Engaging in this personal reflection demands not only unwavering honesty but also profound introspection. It compels you to confront the deep-seated beliefs that obstruct your confidence and creativity in truly meaningful ways, allowing you to redefine your relationship with your artistic expression and to embrace your identity as a creator more fully. To embark on the identification of your triggers, be especially attentive to the moments when you feel inadequate or find yourself questioning your abilities and worth. These feelings might surface during critique sessions, while making unfavorable comparisons with peers, or even when you receive praise for your work, which can often feel undeserved or misplaced. Maintaining a detailed journal can serve as an invaluable tool throughout this process. Diligently note instances where you sense the onset of imposter syndrome, elaborating on the context, your thoughts, and the emotions that arise in those moments. Over time, distinct patterns will emerge, enabling you to pinpoint specific situations or interactions that consistently provoke feelings of self-doubt. This ultimately offers clarity and insight into your experiences and responses, helping you to understand the underlying causes of your feelings and the environmental factors that may influence them. Another highly effective strategy is to seek constructive feedback from trusted colleagues, mentors, or friends within your creative field. Engaging in open discussions about your experiences with others can yield invaluable insights into the triggers you may otherwise overlook or dismiss. These trusted individuals might identify situations where you exhibit self-doubt or anxiety, which you might not even recognize in yourself. This fresh perspective can be enlightening and revealing, serving as a mirror reflecting aspects of your behavior and thought patterns that may need attention. By obtaining this external viewpoint, you can illuminate the sources of your imposter feelings, rendering them more manageable and less isolating. It can thereby foster a sense of community and support among your peers, enhancing your overall experience in the creative space. Sharing your struggles can create a bond that encourages mutual understanding and collaboration, ultimately enriching your creative journey. Once you have successfully identified your triggers, the next critical step is to develop effective and practical strategies for coping with them. This may involve reframing your thoughts when faced with criticism or consciously reminding yourself of your past accomplishments and the unique skills you possess. Techniques such as mindfulness practices, grounding exercises, and even visualization can prove beneficial when you experience overwhelming self-doubt. By actively engaging with your triggers, you can begin to alter your reactions to them, transforming your response to anxiety into proactive strategies for self-empowerment. This transformation allows you to turn moments of anxiety into valuable opportunities for personal growth and development, enhancing your resilience in the face of various challenges that may arise during your creative journey. Ultimately, recognizing and thoroughly understanding your triggers represents a powerful and significant first step toward conquering imposter syndrome. It allows you to reclaim your narrative as an artist and embrace your unique creative journey with renewed confidence and vigor. By engaging in this deep personal reflection, you empower yourself to confront the fears that have held you back for so long, dismantling the barriers that prevent you from achieving your full potential. This fosters the cultivation of a more authentic and confident self-image in your creative endeavors. This ongoing process nurtures personal growth and enriches your artistic expression, leading to a more fulfilling, meaningful, and vibrant creative life. Embracing this journey will undoubtedly enhance not only your personal well-being but also the profound impact of your work on the world around you. This newfound clarity and confidence will allow you to contribute your unique voice and vision more effectively and confidently, making a lasting impression in your field and inspiring others to do the same.

Chapter 3: The Psychological Underpinnings

The Role of Perfectionism

Perfectionism can be an intricate double-edged sword for artists and creatives, serving as both a powerful motivator and a significant barrier to achieving authentic success in their endeavors. On one hand, the unwavering and sometimes relentless pursuit of excellence can inspire individuals to painstakingly refine their craft, driving them to explore innovative techniques, challenge established norms, and expand their creative horizons in remarkably transformative and often unexpected ways. This unwavering commitment to perfection frequently results in the creation of truly extraordinary work that resonates profoundly and meaningfully with audiences, fostering a sincere and deep connection through the medium of art. However, when perfectionism becomes excessive and all-consuming, it can transform into a stifling force that suppresses creativity, breeds feelings of inadequacy, and cultivates a crippling fear of failure that can be particularly overwhelming and difficult to overcome. For numerous artists, the pervasive anxiety of falling short of their own lofty standards can lead to procrastination or, in the most extreme cases, a complete withdrawal from their artistic pursuits altogether. This phenomenon is especially common among those grappling with imposter syndrome, who frequently believe that their artistic creations are unworthy of being shared with the wider world or appreciated by others. The internal narrative often shifts to one dominated by harsh self-criticism, where every perceived flaw is magnified beyond reason, while any achievements are minimized or dismissed altogether, leading to a troubling cycle of self-doubt. This harmful mindset not only obstructs the creative process but also inhibits individuals from fully engaging with their art, ultimately stifling their willingness to share their creations with others. This cyclical pattern of self-doubt can be profoundly damaging, leading to the suppression of one's unique artistic voice and genuine expression. Moreover, perfectionism can create an environment where mistakes are viewed as failures rather than recognized as valuable opportunities for growth, learning, and self-discovery. Many creatives find themselves conditioned to pursue flawless execution, which can result in an unhealthy preoccupation with the final product, diverting their attention away from appreciating the intrinsic journey of creation itself and the joy it can bring. This fixation may culminate in a significant inability to embrace experimentation or risk-taking, both of which are essential and integral components of the creative process that often lead to groundbreaking innovation and transformative ideas. By reframing mistakes as valuable learning experiences, artists can begin to dismantle the rigid constraints imposed by perfectionism, thereby allowing for greater freedom, exploration, and spontaneity in their creative expression and endeavors. To counteract the negative effects of perfectionism, creatives can adopt a range of empowering techniques aimed at fostering a healthier and more balanced relationship with their work and their creative journey. Setting realistic, achievable goals and deadlines can help artists focus on tangible progress rather than becoming ensnared by an unattainable ideal outcome that leads to frustration. Embracing a mindset that prioritizes the notion of "done is better than perfect" encourages individuals to complete projects and actively seek constructive feedback, which can ultimately enhance their skills, foster growth, and boost their confidence in their artistic capabilities. Additionally, practicing self-compassion empowers artists to treat themselves with kindness and understanding, recognizing that personal growth frequently arises from vulnerability and imperfection rather than from an unyielding quest for an impossible ideal of perfection. In summary, while perfectionism may initially seem like a valuable asset in the creative process, it often leads to self-sabotage, persistent feelings of inadequacy, and an overwhelming sense of frustration that can significantly hinder artistic expression. By acknowledging the detrimental aspects of perfectionism and actively implementing effective strategies to overcome its restrictive influence, artists can liberate themselves from the constraints it imposes. This liberation not only fosters a more enjoyable and fulfilling creative experience but also empowers individuals to share their work openly and connect authentically with others in meaningful ways that resonate deeply. Ultimately, this enriches the artistic community as a whole, creating a more inclusive environment that celebrates creativity in all its imperfect and diverse forms, thereby contributing to a richer and more vibrant cultural landscape that benefits everyone involved and inspires future generations of artists. This collective evolution nurtures an atmosphere where creativity is not stifled by unrealistic expectations but rather flourishes through acceptance, collaboration, and shared experiences. In this way, artists can thrive, pushing the boundaries of what is possible while embracing the beauty of imperfection in their creative journeys.

Fear of Failure and Its Consequences

Fear of failure is a pervasive and often debilitating emotion that affects countless individuals, particularly those working in creative fields. This fear can stem from a multitude of sources, including societal pressures, unrealistic personal expectations, and previous negative experiences that linger in the mind, creating a heavy burden. It frequently manifests as a paralyzing anxiety that discourages individuals from taking risks or passionately pursuing their artistic endeavors, trapping them in a cycle of hesitation and self-doubt. The consequences of this fear can be profoundly detrimental, leading to crippling self-doubt, chronic procrastination, and ultimately, a significant reduction in creative output and artistic fulfillment. Understanding and addressing this fear is crucial for those seeking to overcome feelings of imposter syndrome and unlock their true potential as artists. By doing so, they can fully engage with their creative passions without being hindered by crippling fears or debilitating thoughts. One of the most significant and far-reaching consequences of fear of failure is the tendency to avoid challenges altogether. When creative individuals perceive a risk of failure looming ahead, they may instinctively choose to play it safe, opting for familiar paths rather than daring to explore new ideas or innovative techniques that could elevate their work and broaden their horizons. This avoidance behavior can stifle creativity and innovation, preventing artists from discovering their unique voices and styles, which are essential for their growth. Over time, this can lead to stagnation in one's creative journey and a profound disconnection from the joy that comes with authentic artistic expression, leaving individuals feeling unfulfilled and frustrated. Recognizing this detrimental pattern is the crucial first step toward breaking free from the cycle of fear and embracing the myriad possibilities that come with taking calculated risks in their work. Ultimately, this approach fosters a more adventurous and fulfilled creative practice, invigorating their artistic lives by encouraging exploration and experimentation. Additionally, fear of failure often leads to pervasive negative self-talk, which can further entrench feelings of inadequacy and insecurity. Creative individuals may find themselves caught in a relentless loop of comparison, constantly measuring their work against that of others in their field, which can feel overwhelming and discouraging. This self-criticism can be deeply debilitating, fostering an internal narrative that highlights perceived shortcomings and failures rather than celebrating achievements and successes, no matter how small. Such a mindset not only undermines self-esteem but also inhibits collaboration and support within the creative community, creating barriers to connection and understanding. Addressing and reframing these harmful thought patterns is essential for building resilience and confidence in one's unique abilities and creative contributions. By doing this, individuals can ultimately appreciate their work and the value they bring to their art in a more meaningful way, which can significantly enhance their overall artistic experience. Moreover, the impact of fear of failure extends well beyond the individual artist and can significantly affect collaborative projects and team dynamics. When team members are paralyzed by the fear of making mistakes, it creates an atmosphere of tension and a reluctance to share innovative ideas that could benefit the entire group. This stifles creativity and innovation, as open dialogue and experimentation are crucial for artistic growth and development in any collaborative environment. Encouraging a culture that embraces failure as a valuable learning opportunity can foster a more supportive and collaborative environment, allowing artists to take bold and imaginative steps in their work without the overwhelming fear of judgment or criticism from their peers. Such an environment nurtures a sense of community, where risk-taking is viewed not as a personal failing but as a collective journey toward artistic excellence and shared success, ultimately benefiting everyone involved. Ultimately, overcoming the fear of failure requires a multifaceted approach that includes deep self-reflection, reframing perspectives, and building a strong, supportive community that understands the challenges of the creative process. Artists must learn to view failure not as a reflection of their worth or abilities but rather as a necessary part of the intricate creative process that can lead to growth, learning, and self-discovery. Embracing vulnerability and acknowledging that imperfection is inherent in all artistic endeavors can lead to profound personal growth and discovery that enriches the creative journey and expands artistic horizons. By unmasking and confronting the fear of failure, creative individuals can pave the way for authentic expression, meaningful engagement, and fulfillment in their artistic pursuits. This journey ultimately leads to a more enriched and vibrant creative life, where artists can truly thrive in their unique expressions and contribute meaningfully to the broader artistic landscape, fostering connections and inspiring others along the way, creating a ripple effect of creativity and inspiration that benefits the entire community.

Social Comparison and Its Effects

Social comparison serves as a crucial psychological mechanism through which individuals assess their self-worth, skills, and accomplishments by juxtaposing themselves with others within their social milieu. In the vast expanse of creativity, this comparison reveals itself in a multitude of ways, such as evaluating artistic capabilities, analyzing social media engagement, or measuring overall success across diverse fields and disciplines. For many artists and creative individuals, these comparisons can prove especially detrimental, often resulting in feelings of inadequacy, ongoing self-doubt, and a significantly diminished sense of self-esteem. The pervasive influence of social media exacerbates this dilemma, as people are incessantly inundated with carefully curated depictions of others' successes, which frequently lack the essential context that encompasses the hard work, struggles, and sacrifices that underpin those accomplishments. This unrelenting exposure can construct a misleading narrative about what constitutes success and can skew one's understanding of their own unique journey. The ramifications of social comparison on creative professionals can be profoundly impactful and transformative, affecting not only their mindset but also their overall creative output and productivity. When artists gauge their progress against the seemingly flawless achievements of their peers, they may undergo a significant decline in their sense of self-worth and self-confidence. This harmful mindset can ignite feelings of imposter syndrome, where individuals feel like charlatans in their own domain, despite clear evidence of their competence and substantial accomplishments. The stark contrast between one's own reality and the idealized portrayals perpetuated online can generate a toxic cycle of self-criticism and anxiety. This cycle complicates the ability for individuals to create authentic work or engage in creative pursuits with genuine enthusiasm and passion, as they become ensnared in negative thought patterns that hinder their growth. Furthermore, social comparison can lead to a distorted and skewed perception of success. Creatives may start to define their worth exclusively based on external validation, accolades, and recognition from others, rather than finding intrinsic satisfaction in their own work and creative processes. This overwhelming emphasis on external approval can distract individuals from personal goals and authentic creative expression. Ultimately, this shift results in a troubling erosion of passion, motivation, and joy in the creative journey. As individuals become preoccupied with what they believe will earn them approval from others, they may inadvertently suppress their unique voices and visions, leading to homogenized art that lacks personal significance, depth, and authenticity. This unfortunate trend can strip away the individuality that renders art powerful and transformative, reducing its impact. On the flip side, social comparison can also yield positive outcomes if approached in a constructive and mindful manner. By observing the successes of others, creatives can derive valuable inspiration and motivation to enhance their own skills and artistry.

This form of comparison can foster learning, growth, and self-improvement, as artists may feel compelled to broaden their repertoire or delve into new techniques in response to what they admire in others. However, it is essential to maintain a balanced and realistic perspective, acknowledging that everyone's journey is distinct and that external markers of success do not diminish one's own achievements or experiences in any manner. Embracing this perspective empowers artists to appreciate their individual paths while still drawing inspiration from the accomplishments of their peers. To effectively mitigate the adverse impacts of social comparison, creatives can implement several practical strategies that encourage healthier habits and mindsets. Cultivating self-awareness and focusing on personal progress rather than rigid external benchmarks can aid individuals in remaining grounded in their creative pursuits and endeavors. Establishing specific, achievable goals based on personal values and aspirations, rather than succumbing to societal expectations, paves the way for a more fulfilling and rewarding creative practice. In addition, engaging with supportive and encouraging communities can offer a sense of belonging and validation that counters the isolating effects of comparison. Ultimately, by reframing the narrative surrounding social comparison, artists can harness its potential for growth and inspiration while simultaneously safeguarding their mental well-being and creative integrity. This balanced approach can empower individuals to flourish in their creative journeys while appreciating the unique contributions they offer to the artistic landscape.

Chapter 4: The Creative Mindset

Embracing Vulnerability

Embracing vulnerability is not just an essential and transformative step in overcoming imposter syndrome; it is a critical cornerstone of personal and artistic growth, particularly in creative fields where self-expression, authenticity, and individuality are paramount to the artistic journey. Vulnerability involves not only the act of acknowledging our imperfections, fears, and uncertainties but also fully accepting them as intrinsic elements of our humanity. For many artists, the pervasive fear of judgment and the relentless desire for perfection can create a significant barrier that stifles their creativity and inhibits the exploration of new ideas. By recognizing that vulnerability is not a weakness but rather a powerful strength, individuals can cultivate a more genuine and authentic creative process. This vital shift in perspective allows artists to delve deeper into their true selves, enabling them to connect more profoundly with both their work and their audience, thereby enriching the entire creative experience in ways that resonate on multiple levels and foster deeper engagement. To effectively embrace vulnerability, it is crucial to create a safe and supportive space for self-exploration and self-reflection, where individuals feel free to express their thoughts, feelings, and emotions without fear of judgment. This can be achieved through a variety of practices such as journaling, meditation, or engaging in open discussions with trusted peers, mentors, or even support groups. When artists take the time to reflect on their experiences and feelings, they can begin to identify the underlying sources of their imposter syndrome. Understanding these complex emotions helps to demystify the deep-seated fear of inadequacy, making it significantly easier to confront, process, and ultimately transcend them. By cultivating an environment that encourages openness, honesty, and acceptance, artists can dismantle the internal barriers that hinder their creative expression and limit their potential. This supportive atmosphere not only promotes personal growth but also enhances collaboration and shared learning, allowing for richer interactions and exchanges of ideas among creative individuals. Sharing one's work with others can often feel like a daunting and intimidating task, yet it is an incredibly powerful way to embrace vulnerability and foster genuine connection with the world around them. By exposing their creations to the world, artists allow themselves to be seen in their entirety—flaws, struggles, and triumphs included. This courageous act of sharing can foster meaningful connections with others, leading to valuable feedback that contributes significantly to personal and artistic growth. It is essential for artists to remember that not everyone will resonate with their work, and that is perfectly acceptable and completely normal. Engaging with constructive criticism while also celebrating the positive responses can help build confidence and significantly reduce feelings of isolation associated with imposter syndrome. Such interactions can further reinforce the idea that art is subjective and diverse, encouraging artists to explore and express their unique voices without fear of rejection or disapproval. Another vital aspect of embracing vulnerability is the acknowledgment and normalization of the fact that every artist, regardless of their experience level, encounters self-doubt at some point in their journey. This shared commonality can serve as a powerful reminder that they are not alone in their struggles and that self-doubt is a universal experience shared by many. Recognizing that even the most celebrated creatives grapple with feelings of inadequacy can provide much-needed perspective and comfort. By openly sharing these experiences within creative communities, individuals can foster a culture of support, understanding, and empathy, helping to normalize and destigmatize the conversation surrounding vulnerability and self-doubt. This practice of open dialogue can further strengthen community bonds, encouraging emerging artists to seek help and share their feelings without fear of judgment or ridicule from peers or established artists. Ultimately, embracing vulnerability leads to a more authentic, enriching, and fulfilling creative practice that can profoundly transform an artist's approach to their work. When artists allow themselves to be vulnerable, they unlock new avenues of creativity that may have remained hidden, stifled by fear and self-criticism. This openness can inspire innovative ideas, fresh perspectives, and profound connections with their audience that elevate their artistic expression to new heights. By accepting vulnerability as an integral and valuable part of the creative process, artists can confront imposter syndrome head-on and cultivate a deeper sense of self-worth, purpose, and fulfillment in their artistic endeavors. This journey not only enhances their creative output but also enriches their overall experience as artists, leading to greater satisfaction, deeper self-awareness, and significant personal growth that benefits both their art and their lives in meaningful and transformative ways.

The Importance of Self-Compassion

Self-compassion plays an exceptionally crucial role in overcoming imposter syndrome, particularly in creative fields where individuals often grapple with pervasive self-doubt and intense fear of inadequacy. Unlike self-esteem, which is typically contingent upon external validation and achievements that can fluctuate, self-compassion represents a deeper, intrinsic form of support that is not influenced by external circumstances. This intrinsic support emphasizes the importance of treating oneself with kindness during times of struggle and adversity, enabling individuals to cultivate a nurturing and understanding relationship with themselves. Such support acts as a powerful antidote to the crippling effects of imposter syndrome, empowering creatives to navigate their unique challenges with significantly greater resilience and emotional stability. This empowerment facilitates a more profound engagement with their craft and enhances their overall well-being, fostering not just artistic expression but also significant personal growth and development. The practice of self-compassion encompasses three key components: self-kindness, common humanity, and mindfulness. Self-kindness encourages individuals to treat themselves with understanding and care rather than harsh criticism, especially during challenging times or when facing setbacks and failures. Recognizing common humanity fosters the understanding that everyone experiences feelings of failure and inadequacy at various points in their lives. This understanding helps cultivate a sense of connection rather than isolation, reminding individuals that they are not alone in their struggles and that these feelings are a shared human experience. Mindfulness, the third essential component, involves maintaining a balanced awareness of one's emotions and experiences. This awareness allows for the acceptance of difficult feelings without becoming overwhelmed or consumed by them. Together, these elements support a healthier and more constructive mindset, enabling creatives to acknowledge their struggles while also embracing their inherent potential and self-worth, fostering a sense of inner peace, acceptance, and overall well-being that is essential for sustained creativity. In creative pursuits, the pressure to produce exceptional work can significantly exacerbate feelings of inadequacy and self-doubt. Artists, writers, musicians, and other creatives often internalize societal expectations and norms, which can lead to a chronic and paralyzing fear of not meeting those high standards. By actively cultivating self-compassion, individuals can effectively shift their focus from perfectionism to growth and development. This transformative shift allows them to view challenges as valuable opportunities for learning and personal growth rather than as negative reflections of their worth as individuals. When creative individuals consistently practice self-compassion, they are more likely to take meaningful creative risks, experiment with new ideas, and ultimately produce work that is authentic, fulfilling, and true to their unique artistic vision and voice. This leads to a richer and more satisfying creative experience, where the joy of creation can flourish without the constraints of self-doubt and fear, allowing for a more liberated artistic expression. Moreover, self-compassion can significantly enhance emotional regulation, which is vital in creative fields where vulnerability is often a key component of the artistic process. By fostering a compassionate inner dialogue, individuals can better manage feelings of anxiety, fear of failure, and self-doubt that frequently arise in various creative endeavors. This emotional resilience not only aids in overcoming imposter syndrome but also enriches the creative process itself. When artists approach their work with a sense of self-compassion, they create a more welcoming and supportive environment for exploration and self-expression. This environment leads to a deeper and more meaningful engagement with their craft since they feel more liberated to explore their artistic instincts without the weight of self-judgment and fear of failure looming over them, paving the way for innovative ideas and authentic creations. In summary, self-compassion emerges as an essential tool for those grappling with imposter syndrome in creative fields. By nurturing self-kindness, recognizing shared human experiences, and diligently practicing mindfulness, individuals can transform their relationship with themselves and their work in profound ways. This transformation facilitates a more positive and fulfilling creative journey, encouraging individuals to embrace their artistry without the heavy burdens of self-doubt and fear that can stifle creativity. As creatives learn to unmask their true selves through the practice of self-compassion, they pave the way for greater fulfillment and authenticity in their artistic endeavors. Ultimately, this enriches not only their own lives but also the lives of those who experience their unique and powerful work, fostering a more vibrant and supportive creative community that encourages collaboration, innovation, and mutual growth, strengthening connections among artists and audiences alike.

Cultivating a Growth Mindset

Cultivating a growth mindset is not only essential but is also deeply transformative for artists and creatives who grapple with the pervasive feelings associated with imposter syndrome. A growth mindset embodies the empowering belief that abilities and intelligence can be developed, expanded, and refined through dedication, hard work, and an unwavering willingness to learn. This perspective not only fosters resilience but also encourages the valuable lessons that arise from constructive criticism, promoting an enduring love for challenges that push creative boundaries further than ever. When individuals wholeheartedly embrace a growth mindset, they undergo a profound shift in focus, moving from viewing perceived failures as definitive endpoints to recognizing them as rich opportunities for significant growth and development. This mental shift empowers them to navigate the uncertainties and complexities that often accompany creative endeavors with increased ease, confidence, and grace. Such a transformation enhances not only their artistic capabilities but also effectively mitigates the debilitating feelings of inadequacy that many experience on their creative journeys. To actively cultivate a growth mindset, it is paramount to acknowledge and challenge the negative thoughts that contribute to feelings of imposter syndrome. Many creatives internalize self-doubt, often attributing their achievements and successes to mere luck or external circumstances rather than recognizing their own skill, effort, and hard work. Recognizing these pervasive thoughts is the crucial first step toward transforming them into more positive and constructive beliefs. By consciously reframing negative self-talk and replacing it with affirmations of individual capability and potential, artists can begin to view themselves as learners on a continual journey of exploration and improvement rather than as imposters in their own creative spaces. This reframing process not only helps build confidence but also encourages persistence and resilience in the face of inevitable challenges and obstacles that arise along the creative path. Another powerful and effective technique for fostering a growth mindset is the practice of setting realistic and achievable goals that emphasize progress and learning rather than striving for unattainable perfection. By breaking larger projects into smaller, more manageable tasks, artists can create a clear and structured roadmap for improvement that highlights incremental achievements along the way. This method not only allows for a better focus on specific areas of development but also helps in maintaining motivation and enthusiasm throughout the creative process. Celebrating these small victories reinforces the idea that growth is a journey filled with various milestones, which can be especially comforting and motivating during moments of self-doubt and uncertainty. Furthermore, sharing these goals with supportive peers can provide essential accountability and encouragement. This shared experience further reinforces the belief that growth is not only possible but also attainable through collective support and shared experiences within a vibrant creative community, where encouragement can lead to even greater achievements. Feedback is another crucial and indispensable component in the journey of developing a growth mindset. Constructive criticism should be viewed as a valuable tool for improvement, development, and learning rather than as a personal attack that diminishes self-worth or undermines confidence. By actively seeking feedback from trusted mentors, peers, or educators, artists can gain meaningful insights that help them refine their skills, expand their creative horizons, and develop a deeper understanding of their craft. Embracing feedback involves cultivating a genuine willingness to listen and learn from the perspectives of others, which in turn fosters a collaborative and enriching spirit within the creative community. This openness to learning not only enhances artistic abilities but also significantly diminishes the fear of judgment that often accompanies the struggles of imposter syndrome, allowing artists to thrive and flourish in their pursuits. Finally, practicing self-compassion plays a vital and significant role in cultivating a growth mindset that can lead to lasting change and improvement in both personal and professional realms. Recognizing that everyone, regardless of their skill level or experience, encounters setbacks and that making mistakes is a natural and necessary part of the creative process can profoundly help reduce the harsh self-criticism that fuels the fires of imposter syndrome. By treating oneself with kindness, empathy, and understanding during challenging times, artists can create a safe and nurturing space for exploration, experimentation, and risk-taking. This compassionate approach encourages individuals to take creative leaps without the paralyzing fear of failure looming overhead, ultimately leading to greater artistic fulfillment, deeper satisfaction, and a stronger, more resilient belief in their own capabilities and potential. This journey toward embracing a growth mindset is not just beneficial but essential for artists seeking to thrive in their creative expressions and endeavors, allowing them to continuously evolve and innovate in their work.

Chapter 5: Techniques for Overcoming Imposter Syndrome

Cognitive Behavioral Strategies

Cognitive Behavioral Strategies (CBT) provide a comprehensive and structured framework to effectively address the enduring emotions linked to imposter syndrome, a phenomenon particularly prevalent in creative industries. Central to CBT is the crucial awareness that our thoughts, emotions, and behaviors are intricately connected, each significantly impacting the others. By focusing on the transformation of maladaptive thought patterns, individuals can notably reduce feelings of anxiety while cultivating a deeper sense of self-confidence in their capabilities and potential. This subchapter will delve into practical cognitive behavioral strategies carefully crafted to support artists and creatives in identifying, confronting, and ultimately overcoming persistent feelings of inadequacy. Empowering individuals in this manner allows them to embrace their unique talents fully and contribute meaningfully to their artistic and creative pursuits. One particularly effective cognitive behavioral strategy is cognitive restructuring. This process involves identifying negative thought patterns and systematically replacing them with more realistic and positive alternatives. For instance, an artist might struggle with the belief, "I am not as talented as my peers," which can lead to overwhelming self-doubt and insecurity. By challenging this detrimental thought and actively considering evidence of their own achievements, skills, and unique qualities, the artist can shift their perspective toward something more affirming, such as, "I possess unique strengths and experiences that enrich my artistic voice and vision." This cognitive shift not only alleviates feelings of inadequacy but also fosters a healthier and more positive self-image. It empowers the individual to recognize and appreciate their worth within the creative landscape, thus enhancing their overall artistic journey and creative expression. Another invaluable technique within this framework is the practice of self-compassion. Individuals grappling with imposter syndrome often engage in harsh self-criticism, which exacerbates feelings of unworthiness and self-doubt. By nurturing self-compassion, artists learn to treat themselves with the same kindness and understanding they would naturally extend to a friend facing similar challenges and difficulties. This may involve acknowledging that everyone makes mistakes and that encountering setbacks and moments of uncertainty is entirely natural. Regularly practicing self-compassion can greatly assist creatives in cultivating a healthier relationship with both their work and themselves. This approach effectively alleviates the oppressive burden of imposter feelings and creates pathways for greater self-acceptance and personal growth, enabling artists to flourish in their creative endeavors. Behavioral activation stands out as another strategy that can be particularly beneficial for individuals experiencing imposter syndrome. This technique encourages individuals to actively engage in activities they find enjoyable or fulfilling, effectively counteracting feelings of avoidance and withdrawal that often accompany self-doubt and insecurity. For example, a writer who feels like a fraud may avoid writing altogether, which only reinforces their negative beliefs and further entraps them in a damaging cycle of self-doubt. By setting small, achievable goals—such as dedicating just ten minutes each day to writing—they can gradually reconnect with their craft and creative expression. This incremental approach not only sharpens their writing skills but also builds confidence over time, helping to dismantle the self-perpetuating cycle of avoidance and debilitating self-doubt, ultimately leading to a more gratifying and fulfilling creative life. Through these strategies, artists can discover renewed motivation and joy in their work, allowing them to thrive in their creative journeys. By implementing these techniques, they can transform their experience, breaking free from the confines of self-doubt and embracing their full potential. Finally, the practice of journaling can serve as an exceptionally powerful and transformative tool within the context of cognitive behavioral strategies and personal growth. Maintaining a journal provides creatives with the invaluable opportunity to document their thoughts and feelings, offering a dedicated space for thoughtful reflection and thorough analysis. By writing about their experiences with imposter syndrome, artists can more effectively identify recurring themes, patterns, and triggers that contribute to their feelings of inadequacy and self-criticism. This practice not only promotes a heightened sense of self-awareness but also facilitates the development of personalized coping strategies that are specifically tailored to their unique experiences and challenges. Over time, consistent journaling can lead to a deeper understanding of one's creative journey, while also fostering a more resilient and robust mindset. This ongoing process enables artists to confront their feelings of imposter syndrome with enhanced clarity, strength, and renewed confidence in both their abilities and artistic vision. Ultimately, it allows them to embrace their creative potential more fully and authentically, unlocking new avenues for self-expression and innovation. Additionally, journaling provides a structured way to track progress, celebrate small victories, and navigate the inevitable ups and downs of the artistic process, reinforcing the notion that every artist's journey is valid and worthy of exploration. It encourages individuals to reflect on their aspirations, challenges, and growth, creating a holistic view of their artistic path. Through this iterative process, artists become more equipped to handle setbacks and recognize the value in their experiences, ultimately cultivating a profound appreciation for their unique contributions to the creative landscape. This enriched understanding not only enhances their artistic practice but also deepens their connection to their own narratives, allowing for a more fulfilling and meaningful engagement with their work.

Mindfulness and Meditation Practices

Mindfulness and meditation practices serve as exceptionally powerful tools for artists and creatives grappling with feelings of imposter syndrome, which can often hinder their ability to fully express themselves and tap into their creative potential. By cultivating a heightened awareness of the present moment, individuals can foster a much deeper connection to their creative process while significantly reducing the anxiety that often accompanies overwhelming self-doubt and insecurity. These practices actively encourage a meaningful shift in focus from seeking external validation to nurturing internal acceptance, which is crucial for personal growth and development. This important shift empowers artists to recognize their intrinsic worth and unique contributions without the persistent comparison to others that can often stifle creativity and innovation, allowing their true artistic voices to emerge more freely and authentically. Meditation, in particular, offers a variety of techniques that can be customized to suit individual preferences and lifestyles, making it accessible to everyone, regardless of their background or experience level. Simple practices such as breath awareness meditation can effectively help quiet the mind and create ample space for creativity to flourish and thrive. By dedicating just a few minutes each day to focus on the breath and the sensations of inhalation and exhalation, artists can develop a profound sense of calm and clarity that permeates their creative endeavors. This state of mind can be instrumental in countering the negative self-talk that often accompanies imposter syndrome, transforming the artist's approach to their work and allowing them to engage with their creative process in a more meaningful and fulfilling way. Regular meditation can also enhance concentration and focus, making it significantly easier for creatives to engage fully and wholeheartedly with their work while navigating the complexities of their artistic journeys and the multitude of challenges they face along the way. Mindfulness, on the other hand, involves being completely present in the moment, whether during the creative process or in the flow of daily life. This practice encourages individuals to observe their thoughts and feelings without judgment, thereby helping to diminish feelings of inadequacy and self-criticism that can be debilitating for many artists. By embracing mindfulness, creatives can learn to appreciate their unique creative journeys in all their forms, recognizing that self-doubt is a common experience shared by many rather than a personal failing unique to them. This significant perspective shift can empower individuals to take risks and experiment boldly in their work, leading to valuable growth, innovation, and the development of a more authentic artistic voice that resonates with their true self and aspirations, ultimately enriching their artistic expression in profound ways. Moreover, integrating mindfulness into creative routines can notably enhance both productivity and overall satisfaction, enriching the creative process in a manner that feels both natural and fulfilling. When artists focus on the creative process rather than solely on the end result, they may find themselves feeling more engaged, inspired, and alive in their work. Techniques such as mindful walking, drawing, or even engaging with nature can serve as enriching gateways to creativity, encouraging individuals to explore their surroundings or express their thoughts in fresh, new ways that reflect their personal experiences and insights. By valuing the act of creation itself and immersing themselves in the moment, artists can effectively diminish the pressure of expectations that often contribute to the distress of imposter syndrome, creating an environment in which their creativity can thrive without constraints or limitations. This holistic approach not only nurtures their artistic talents but also enriches their personal experiences and overall well-being, fostering a sense of balance and fulfillment in their lives while allowing their creativity to flourish unencumbered by doubt. In conclusion, mindfulness and meditation practices provide not only essential but also transformative strategies for artists who are striving to overcome the myriad challenges posed by imposter syndrome. This syndrome can often feel overwhelmingly pervasive, deeply impacting their confidence and sense of self-worth in profound ways. By cultivating self-awareness and fostering a genuine sense of acceptance, these practices can lead to significant and life-changing transformations in the creative experience for artists. They empower individuals to embrace their identity as artists more fully and authentically, allowing for a much richer and deeper engagement with their work. As artists learn to navigate their thoughts and feelings with compassion and understanding, they can cultivate a remarkable resilience and discover newfound confidence that propels their creative journey forward. This transformative journey ultimately helps to unmask their true potential and reveals the vast array of possibilities that lie ahead in their unique artistic paths. Such empowerment inspires them to pursue their passions with renewed vigor and creativity, driving them to explore new avenues of expression and innovation. It instills a profound sense of inspiration and a deep, unwavering commitment to their craft that genuinely reflects their authentic selves. In turn, this leads to a more vibrant, meaningful, and fulfilling artistic life, where they can express their true essence freely and make a lasting impact through their work, enriching not only their own lives but also the lives of those who experience their creations.

Setting Realistic Goals and Expectations

Setting realistic goals and expectations is not merely an essential step; it stands as a critical and foundational aspect of overcoming imposter syndrome, particularly in creative fields where self-doubt can often feel like an unshakeable companion that clings persistently. Artists, writers, and various creators frequently find themselves grappling with overwhelming feelings of inadequacy, often convinced that their work consistently falls short of their own high standards or that they are unworthy of the accolades and accomplishments they have painstakingly achieved throughout their journeys. By establishing achievable and well-defined goals, individuals can create a structured path forward that not only significantly boosts their confidence but also effectively mitigates the pervasive feelings of inadequacy that can hinder their creative expression. Realistic goals provide a vital framework that empowers creatives to evaluate their progress, celebrate even the smallest victories along the way, and gradually nurture a sense of self-efficacy and belonging within their respective fields. This ongoing process fosters a more profound and meaningful connection to their artistic identities and instills a greater sense of purpose in their creative endeavors, enabling them to thrive in their pursuits and navigate the complexities of the creative landscape. To begin the comprehensive and transformative process of setting realistic goals, it is essential to dedicate ample time for deep and thoughtful reflection on personal strengths and weaknesses. Gaining a deeper understanding of one's unique creative capabilities and limitations can greatly inform the crafting of goals that are both ambitious and attainable in nature, striking a balance between aspiration and realism. For instance, while a writer may dream of completing an entire novel within a single year, a more practical and manageable approach might involve setting a specific goal to consistently write a certain number of words each day, such as 500 or 1,000, depending on individual circumstances, personal commitments, and available time. This incremental strategy not only alleviates pressure but also provides ample room for necessary adjustments and refinements along the way. By focusing on manageable tasks, creatives can maintain their motivation and experience steady, tangible progress, which is crucial for effectively tackling the complexities of imposter syndrome and cultivating a healthy, sustainable creative practice that allows for growth, exploration, and the development of one's unique voice in their artistry. Another essential aspect of effective goal-setting is ensuring that the objectives are not only specific, measurable, and clearly defined but also realistic and achievable within a given timeframe. Vague or ambiguous goals can often lead to significant frustration and an increased sense of failure, which can further amplify feelings of inadequacy and self-doubt among individuals. Instead of merely expressing a general desire to "become a better artist," a more constructive and actionable goal could be articulated as "attend one art workshop each month," "complete three new pieces of artwork by the end of the current season," or even "experiment with a new medium every two months." By articulating goals in clear, concrete terms, individuals are in a much better position to track their achievements and gather tangible evidence of their growth. This evidence reinforces a genuine sense of accomplishment and intrinsic worth, creating a positive feedback loop that enhances motivation and drives further progress. This process not only elevates their confidence in their creative abilities but also helps create a more positive and empowering mindset surrounding their artistic journey. This shift in perspective allows for greater exploration and experimentation in their art, ultimately leading to richer and more fulfilling creative experiences that resonate deeply with their personal vision. Moreover, it is crucial to remain flexible and open to the notion of recalibrating goals in response to evolving circumstances and life's inherent unpredictability. Creative endeavors often demand a high degree of adaptability and resilience. Embracing the idea that goals can evolve over time empowers individuals to navigate challenges without the added burden of perceived failure or disillusionment. For instance, if a personal situation arises that limits the time available for creative work, it is entirely reasonable and appropriate to adjust the timeline for project completion. This could involve extending deadlines, allowing for more breathing room, or refocusing efforts on smaller, more manageable projects that can be completed within the new constraints. This adaptability not only showcases resilience but also fosters a healthier relationship with creativity, where the emphasis is balanced between the journey of creation and the end result. Ultimately, this approach leads to a more fulfilling and enriching artistic experience, allowing individuals to appreciate their growth fully and celebrate their creative expressions in a more meaningful and profound way. This appreciation fosters a deep sense of pride in their artistic journey and the unique contributions they can offer to the broader artistic community, reinforcing their connection to the larger narrative of creativity and collaboration. Ultimately, setting realistic goals and expectations serves as a powerful tool in the ongoing battle against imposter syndrome, which many artists face at various points in their careers. By constructing a supportive framework for both personal growth and professional development, individuals can cultivate a more positive self-image while simultaneously diminishing feelings of fraudulence and self-doubt that can hinder their progress and undermine their self-worth. As they achieve their goals, regardless of how small they may appear, they will gradually internalize their successes and come to recognize their rightful place within the broader creative community. This transformative journey not only enhances their craft but also empowers them to fully embrace their identities as artists, liberated from the constraints of self-doubt and insecurity that often plague creative minds. Through this process, they can build a lasting foundation of confidence that allows them to thrive creatively and boldly express their unique vision. Ultimately, this leads to richer, more fulfilling artistic expressions and deeper connections with their audience and fellow creators. This journey of self-discovery and validation is crucial in nurturing a sustainable, joyful, and impactful creative life while fostering a sense of belonging and purpose in their artistic endeavors. It helps them to feel connected not just to their work but to the vibrant community of artists who share similar struggles and aspirations.

Chapter 6: Building a Supportive Community

The Power of Peer Support

Peer support plays an exceptionally vital role in assisting individuals as they navigate the intricate complexities of imposter syndrome, particularly within creative fields. This challenging phenomenon frequently leads artists to doubt their own abilities, feel unworthy of the achievements they have accomplished, and harbor a persistent and often overwhelming fear of being exposed as a fraud. By fostering meaningful connections with peers who share similar experiences and challenges, individuals can cultivate a supportive environment that actively encourages vulnerability, openness, and honest discourse about their feelings. This connection not only normalizes the often-overwhelming feelings of self-doubt but also reinforces the notion that such emotions are not unique to one person but rather common among creatives, thereby significantly reducing the isolation that frequently accompanies the experience of imposter syndrome. The shared experience of these feelings fosters a profound sense of belonging, reminding artists that they are part of a larger community grappling with similar challenges and struggles. The exchange of experiences among peers can be incredibly validating and affirming. When artists come together to discuss their struggles with feelings of inadequacy and self-doubt, they often discover, to their relief and sometimes surprise, that others face remarkably similar challenges and uncertainties. This shared understanding effectively helps to dismantle the pervasive myth of the "lone genius" and highlights the undeniable reality that creativity is rarely a solitary journey, but rather a collective endeavor enriched by collaboration and mutual support. By actively engaging in conversations that acknowledge and validate these feelings, artists can gain much-needed perspective and realize that their self-doubt does not diminish their inherent talent or worth as individuals in any way. This validation can serve as a powerful catalyst for transformative change, empowering individuals to confront their fears head-on and take ownership of their unique creative identities and contributions. Embracing this collective experience can lead to a deeper appreciation of one's artistic journey, fostering resilience in the face of adversity and encouraging a stronger commitment to personal growth. Moreover, peer support networks can provide an array of practical strategies for overcoming the debilitating effects of imposter syndrome. Collaborating with fellow artists often leads to the sharing of effective techniques and coping mechanisms that have proven successful in managing self-doubt and anxiety. Whether through structured workshops, mentorship programs, or informal meetups, these interactions promote a rich culture of continuous learning, collaboration, and personal growth. Artists can exchange constructive feedback, share valuable resources, and offer much-needed encouragement, fostering an atmosphere where individuals feel safe and encouraged to explore bold new ideas and take creative risks. This collective wisdom can be instrumental in helping artists build resilience against the pressures and challenges associated with imposter syndrome, creating a strong foundation for ongoing artistic development. The diverse perspectives offered within these networks can also inspire innovative approaches to creative challenges, greatly enriching the overall artistic experience and enabling artists to expand their horizons. Another significant aspect of peer support is the crucial element of accountability that it introduces into the creative process. When artists forge meaningful connections with one another, they often experience a heightened sense of responsibility to actively pursue and achieve their creative goals. This accountability can manifest in a variety of productive ways, such as setting concrete deadlines for projects or committing to regular check-ins with peers to discuss both progress and challenges. By establishing these expectations, artists become far less likely to succumb to crippling self-doubt or procrastination, as they recognize that their peers are genuinely invested in their success and well-being. This external motivation can substantially assist individuals in pushing through barriers, ultimately leading to increased productivity and a more profound sense of accomplishment and fulfillment in their artistic endeavors. The encouragement that stems from accountability can also foster a sense of camaraderie, further motivating artists to strive toward their aspirations with renewed vigor and enthusiasm. This dynamic can create an enriching cycle of support and progress that enhances both individual and collective artistic journeys, making peer support an invaluable resource in the creative process and an essential component of thriving in the arts. In conclusion, the power of peer support truly cannot be overstated in the ongoing journey of overcoming imposter syndrome within the diverse and dynamic realm of creative fields. By creating a robust network that is rich in understanding, empathy, and a wealth of shared experiences, artists can find immense solace in the comforting knowledge that they are not alone in their struggles and challenges. Through the process of validation, the exchange of practical strategies, and a strong sense of accountability, peer support provides invaluable resources for individuals who are actively seeking to conquer their self-doubt and ultimately thrive in their creative endeavors. Cultivating these enriching connections not only enhances individual artistic practices but also significantly strengthens the creative community as a whole. This fosters an environment where all artists can thrive, grow, and flourish together in their unique expressions and perspectives. Emphasizing collaboration and the sharing of experiences not only enhances the richness of the creative landscape but also paves the way for a vibrant, interconnected, and supportive artistic ecosystem that benefits everyone involved. Furthermore, it ensures that artists feel empowered to explore their creativity without fear of judgment, reinforcing the idea that every voice matters and contributes to the overall tapestry of the artistic community, ultimately creating a more inclusive and diverse environment that celebrates the unique contributions of each individual. Through this collaborative spirit, artists not only support each other but also inspire one another to reach new heights in their creative journeys, fostering a culture of innovation and mutual respect that can lead to profound artistic breakthroughs and a deeper understanding of the creative process itself.

Finding Mentors and Role Models

Finding mentors and role models is not just an essential but also a transformative step in overcoming imposter syndrome, particularly in creative fields where self-doubt frequently acts as a significant barrier to both personal and professional growth. Mentors offer invaluable guidance, unwavering support, and a wealth of experience that can empower individuals to successfully navigate their unique artistic journeys with newfound confidence and clarity. They provide crucial insights into the multifaceted challenges of the creative process, validate feelings of inadequacy, and share their own personal experiences with imposter syndrome, which can be incredibly reassuring and encouraging for those who grapple with similar feelings. By observing the diverse paths taken by their mentors, aspiring artists can develop a much clearer understanding of what genuine success truly looks like, recognizing that it often comes with its own set of challenges, struggles, and inevitable setbacks. Such success frequently demands resilience, adaptability, and the courage to overcome the hurdles that arise along the way, which can often feel daunting without the proper support. To initiate the search for mentors, individuals should thoughtfully consider and reflect on their existing networks and communities. This exploration might involve reaching out to local art organizations, attending workshops, or actively participating in online forums dedicated to various creative pursuits and interests. Networking events can prove particularly valuable, as they create excellent opportunities to connect with seasoned professionals who are eager to share their extensive knowledge and experiences with those who seek guidance. Engaging in meaningful and sincere conversations with those who inspire you can lead to fruitful relationships that have the potential to evolve into long-lasting mentorships, enriching both parties involved. It is vital to approach potential mentors with genuine curiosity, respect, and a clear acknowledgment of their time and expertise, as this sets a positive tone for the relationship and fosters mutual appreciation, trust, and understanding. In addition to establishing formal mentorship relationships, role models can also play a significant role in combating feelings of inadequacy and persistent self-doubt. These figures do not necessarily need to be one-on-one mentors; they can be accomplished artists, influential authors, or respected industry leaders whose work resonates deeply with you and inspires you to reach higher and aim further. By studying their diverse journeys and career trajectories, individuals can uncover a variety of strategies that these role models employed to overcome the numerous challenges they faced throughout their careers. This process can serve as a powerful and ongoing source of inspiration, continually reminding aspiring artists that success is rarely linear and often demands perseverance, consistent practice, and unwavering resilience in the face of adversity. Additionally, it encourages the courage to embrace failure as a necessary stepping stone to growth, turning setbacks into valuable learning experiences that contribute to overall artistic development. When actively seeking out mentors and role models, it is highly beneficial to set specific, tangible goals regarding what you hope to achieve from the relationship. These objectives could encompass gaining constructive feedback on your work, learning about the intricacies of the industry, or developing a stronger and more authentic artistic voice that truly reflects your individual self and vision. Clearly communicating these objectives can significantly assist both the mentor and the mentee in establishing a productive and supportive dynamic that fosters mutual growth, understanding, and respect. Additionally, being open to constructive criticism and demonstrating a genuine willingness to learn from the experiences of others can greatly enhance personal growth and development across various creative pursuits. This proactive approach provides invaluable insights that might otherwise remain untapped and overlooked, ultimately enriching the artistic journey and empowering individuals to reach their fullest potential while navigating the complexities of their creative endeavors in a truly meaningful way, fostering resilience and adaptability in the face of challenges. It is crucial to remember that mentorship is a two-way street. While seeking guidance and support is undeniably important for your growth and development, contributing to the relationship by sharing your own insights, experiences, and unique talents can greatly enrich the process for both parties involved. Actively engaging with mentors and role models in a meaningful and reciprocal way can cultivate a vibrant sense of community and collaboration, enhancing the overall experience for everyone involved in this creative exchange. As individuals continue to evolve in their artistic endeavors, they may also find themselves inspired to become mentors to others, thereby creating a continuous cycle of support and encouragement that helps to diminish feelings of imposter syndrome within the broader creative community. This cultivation of mentorship not only fosters personal and professional development but also creates an environment where everyone can thrive and flourish together, benefiting from a wealth of shared knowledge and experiences. Such interconnectedness ultimately strengthens the creative community, encouraging all individuals to pursue their passions with greater confidence, authenticity, and a shared sense of purpose that transcends individual limitations. In addition, it can be immensely valuable to reflect on the specific qualities you admire in potential mentors, as this can guide your search and inform your conversations. Whether you are looking for someone with particular expertise, a unique perspective, or a similar background, identifying these traits can help you approach the right individuals with clear intentions and focused energy.

Furthermore, the process of mentorship can also provide opportunities for networking, as mentors often have extensive connections within the industry that can open doors and pave the way for new collaborations and innovative projects. By nurturing these relationships, you not only gain insights and guidance but also become part of a larger network of creative professionals who can support each other's aspirations. Embracing this collaborative spirit can lead to enriching experiences, inspiring projects, and profound artistic growth, as you and your mentors navigate the ever-evolving landscape of creativity together, ultimately creating an ecosystem where creativity thrives and flourishes beyond individual efforts. This collaborative network not only amplifies individual voices but also creates a shared platform for innovation, allowing the creative community to explore new horizons and push boundaries collectively, reinforcing the idea that mentorship is a vital catalyst for both personal and communal growth.

Creating Safe Spaces for Sharing

Creating safe spaces for sharing is absolutely essential for artists and creatives who grapple with the pervasive and often debilitating effects of imposter syndrome. These specially designed environments foster a nurturing and supportive atmosphere where individuals feel entirely comfortable expressing their thoughts, innovative ideas, and deep vulnerabilities without the looming fear of judgment or criticism that often stifles creativity and personal expression. Establishing such an inclusive atmosphere can significantly enhance not just individual creativity but also collaboration among peers, leading to richer artistic experiences and deeper, more meaningful connections that can resonate profoundly in their work. Safe spaces actively encourage open dialogue, allowing participants to explore their insecurities in a supportive context while receiving validation and understanding from others who may share similar challenges and experiences. This sense of belonging can be transformative, enabling individuals to flourish creatively and authentically, unlocking their potential in ways they may not have previously imagined or believed possible, ultimately leading to innovative artistic breakthroughs. To create a truly effective safe space, it is crucial to establish a comprehensive set of ground rules that promote respect, confidentiality, and active listening among all participants involved. This can be achieved by setting clear and thorough expectations at the outset of discussions or workshops, ensuring that everyone understands the shared commitment to fostering a positive and productive environment. Encouraging participants to focus on providing constructive feedback rather than engaging in any form of criticism can greatly aid in nurturing a positive and affirming atmosphere where everyone feels safe to participate. Furthermore, incorporating engaging icebreaker activities can significantly ease participants into sharing openly, helping them develop a sense of comfort and trust with one another from the very beginning. When individuals feel respected, valued, and truly heard, they become more inclined to open up about their fears and challenges related to their creative pursuits, fostering deeper connections that enhance their work in extraordinary ways and providing a solid foundation for collaboration that can lead to remarkable outcomes, both individually and collectively. Another vital aspect of creating safe spaces is ensuring that diversity and inclusivity are always at the forefront of the initiative. A genuinely diverse group brings a wealth of varied perspectives and lived experiences that can greatly enrich discussions and fuel creativity in unexpected and inspiring ways. When individuals from different backgrounds come together, they have the invaluable opportunity to share unique insights and stories that may deeply resonate with others who often feel isolated in their experiences. Promoting inclusivity actively helps dismantle stereotypes and biases that frequently contribute to feelings of inadequacy, ultimately allowing all participants to feel genuinely valued and understood within the group dynamic. This shared understanding can lead to collaboration and innovation, resulting in distinct and powerful artistic expressions that might not have been possible in a less inclusive environment, thereby broadening the horizons of creativity for everyone involved. Additionally, it fosters a richer artistic community that thrives on collaboration and mutual respect, encouraging each member to contribute their unique voice and perspective, which in turn enhances the collective artistic dialogue. Facilitators play an indispensable role in maintaining the safety and integrity of these vital spaces. They should be trained in a variety of techniques that promote empathy, understanding, and effective communication, allowing them to navigate sensitive topics with both care and skill. A skilled and attentive facilitator can help manage group dynamics, ensuring that everyone has an opportunity to participate while also addressing any disruptive behaviors that may arise during discussions. By fostering a supportive and encouraging atmosphere, facilitators can empower participants to confront their imposter syndrome head-on, motivating them to share their unique creative journeys and personal stories more openly and authentically. This empowerment can lead to transformative experiences for all involved, opening doors to new perspectives and artistic growth that can reverberate far beyond the confines of the immediate space. Such growth creates lasting impacts that enrich the broader creative landscape and inspire future generations of artists and innovators, allowing them to build upon the foundations laid by those who came before. Finally, it is absolutely essential to recognize that creating and maintaining safe spaces is not just a one-time effort but rather an ongoing and evolving process that requires unwavering commitment, active participation, and adaptability from all individuals involved in the community. Regular check-ins can provide invaluable insights into the comfort levels of participants, helping to identify and address any emerging issues effectively and promptly, thus ensuring that everyone feels secure, respected, and valued. Encouraging open feedback about the space itself not only guides necessary improvements but also reinforces the critical importance of safety in the realm of creative sharing. This fosters an environment where individuals can express themselves freely and authentically, without fear of judgment or repercussion. By committing to the continuous development and nurturing of these safe spaces, artists and creatives can cultivate a thriving community where vulnerability is not only embraced but celebrated, ultimately leading to profound personal growth and enhanced artistic expression for all those involved. This journey of growth can enrich not only individual experiences but also significantly strengthen the collective creative landscape, making it more vibrant, dynamic, and inclusive for everyone involved. It fosters a powerful sense of unity and collaboration that transcends individual crafts and disciplines, allowing diverse voices to harmonize beautifully in a shared pursuit of artistic excellence and innovation. Such a collaborative effort creates a rich tapestry of creativity that truly reflects the depth and richness of the human experience. This benefits the entire community of artists and their audiences alike, while simultaneously inspiring future generations to continue this invaluable legacy of inclusivity, creativity, and mutual support, ensuring that the artistic community remains a nurturing and empowering space for all.

Chapter 7: Celebrating Achievements

Acknowledging Your Successes

Acknowledging your successes is not just an essential step; it represents a transformative journey in overcoming imposter syndrome, particularly for those deeply immersed in creative fields. Many individuals often wrestle with the inclination to downplay their achievements, attributing them to mere luck or external circumstances rather than fully recognizing their own skills, talent, and hard work. This harmful pattern of thinking not only stifles self-confidence but also significantly impedes both personal and professional growth. By actively recognizing and celebrating your successes, you can initiate a powerful shift in your mindset, reinforcing your self-worth and validating the invaluable contributions you make in your artistic and creative endeavors. Acknowledgment of success is crucial for building a positive self-image and can lead to a greater sense of fulfillment in your creative journey, allowing you to embrace your identity as an artist with pride. One highly effective method to acknowledge your successes is through the practice of self-reflection. Dedicate time to thoughtfully evaluate your achievements, regardless of whether they are big or small. Create a comprehensive list that encompasses completed projects, positive feedback received from peers or clients, and significant milestones reached throughout your creative journey. This tangible record serves as a powerful reminder of your capabilities and the inherent value you bring to your field. Regularly revisiting this list not only combats feelings of inadequacy but also serves as a constant reminder that your accomplishments are not merely coincidental or the result of external factors but rather a testament to your hard work and dedication. This ongoing practice of reflection, when integrated into your routine, can open doors to a deeper understanding of your growth and untapped potential, allowing you to see how far you have come and where you can go next, ultimately revealing the breadth of your artistic journey. Another valuable technique is to share your successes with others. Engaging in meaningful conversations about your achievements with friends, colleagues, or mentors can provide invaluable external validation and support. This social reinforcement helps normalize the recognition of accomplishments and can inspire others to adopt the same practice. When you vocalize your successes, it not only solidifies them in your mind but also fosters a culture of appreciation and encouragement within your creative community. This creates an environment where everyone feels empowered to celebrate their own wins and achievements, thus enhancing collective morale and motivation, which can lead to greater collaboration and innovative ideas. The act of sharing not only amplifies your own confidence but also contributes to a supportive network where mutual encouragement thrives, allowing for a sense of camaraderie that benefits all. In addition to reflection and sharing, setting specific, well-defined goals can further enhance your ability to acknowledge success. By establishing clear, measurable objectives, you create a structured pathway for achievement that can be celebrated and recognized. Each time you reach a goal, no matter how minor it may seem, take the time to genuinely acknowledge it and appreciate the effort that led to this success. This practice builds a consistent pattern of recognition, reinforcing your progress and helping to diminish feelings of imposter syndrome over time. Celebrating these victories, regardless of their size, contributes to a more robust and resilient sense of identity as an artist and creative individual, enabling you to approach future challenges with renewed strength and confidence. Acknowledging both small wins and larger accomplishments fosters a sense of continuity in your development as a creative professional, empowering you to pursue your goals with fervor and resilience. Finally, it is absolutely essential to cultivate a mindset of gratitude, both for your successes and for the journey that has led you to where you are today. Recognizing the hard work, dedication, and perseverance that have fueled your accomplishments can dramatically shift your focus from self-doubt to genuine appreciation. A mindset of gratitude helps ground you in the present moment, allowing you to fully embrace your achievements without the overshadowing influence of imposter syndrome lingering in the background. By fostering this positive mindset, you empower yourself to acknowledge your successes wholeheartedly and move forward confidently in your creative pursuits, fully prepared to tackle new challenges and seize exciting opportunities that lie ahead. This journey of celebrating yourself not only enhances your personal growth but also contributes to a vibrant and thriving creative community. Embracing gratitude and recognizing your journey allows you to inspire others, creating a ripple effect that uplifts everyone involved in the creative process.

Keeping a Success Journal

Keeping a success journal is an exceptionally powerful technique for combating imposter syndrome, particularly in creative fields where self-doubt can frequently loom large and become overwhelming. This empowering practice involves not only documenting every achievement, no matter how small, trivial, or seemingly insignificant it might appear, but also taking the time to reflect deeply on personal growth and development over time. By regularly noting successes, individuals can cultivate a tangible and inspiring record of their capabilities and accomplishments, which serves as a vital reminder of their skills, talents, and the hard work that has led them to where they are today. This practice can be especially beneficial for artists, writers, and other creatives who often find themselves grappling with self-doubt and the pervasive fear of being exposed as a fraud. Such feelings can hinder their confidence and creative expression, stifling their ability to innovate and share their unique perspectives with the world and art forms they cherish. The process of maintaining a success journal is straightforward yet profoundly impactful, offering a simple yet meaningful way to track progress and growth over time. Start by choosing a medium that feels comfortable and accessible to you, whether it be a traditional physical notebook, a digital online document, or even a dedicated app designed specifically for journaling and self-reflection. Each entry should include specific details about the achievement, including the date, the nature of the accomplishment, and any relevant context surrounding it. This could range from completing a challenging and demanding project to receiving positive feedback from peers, or even overcoming significant personal obstacles that once seemed insurmountable. Regularly revisiting these entries can provide reassurance, motivation, and a much-needed boost to self-esteem, reinforcing the notion that success is not an isolated incident but rather a consistent pattern that reflects ongoing growth, resilience, and perseverance in one's creative journey, allowing individuals to recognize their progress more clearly and appreciate the journey they have undertaken. In addition to recording successes, it is equally important to take the time to reflect on the emotions and thoughts that accompany these achievements. This reflection can help individuals better understand their triggers for self-doubt and feelings of being an imposter, allowing them to confront these feelings head-on with greater awareness and understanding. By analyzing how they felt at the moment of success—whether it was joy, disbelief, pride, or even guilt—creatives can begin to identify and challenge the negative narratives that often arise in their minds, narratives that can undermine their confidence and sense of belonging in their artistic communities. This reflective practice fosters a deeper level of self-awareness and encourages a meaningful transformation in mindset, allowing individuals to embrace their accomplishments rather than dismiss them as unworthy or insignificant. Dismissing these achievements can often happen in the face of pervasive self-doubt that clouds their perception of success and fulfillment, leading to a cycle of negative self-talk that further erodes their confidence and creative potential. To maximize the benefits of a success journal, it is highly advisable to set aside dedicated and intentional time each week specifically for the purpose of reviewing and updating it. This routine not only reinforces the vital habit of recognizing and celebrating achievements but also creates a valuable space for self-reflection and deep contemplation. Engaging in such practices can lead to profound insights regarding one's creative process and personal growth. During these dedicated sessions, individuals can identify recurring patterns in their successes, whether they be specific skills they excel in or projects that resonate deeply with them, effectively igniting their passion for creativity. These insights can serve as a guiding light for future creative endeavors, significantly bolstering confidence in their artistic identity and abilities. This newfound confidence enables them to pursue their passions with greater boldness, determination, and clarity. Ultimately, this enriching practice enhances their creative lives while fostering a profound sense of fulfillment, allowing them to navigate the diverse landscape of creativity with renewed vigor, assurance, and an unwavering belief in their unique contributions to the world around them. Maintaining a success journal also serves as an empowering tool for creatives who are grappling with the often-challenging experiences of imposter syndrome. By consistently documenting and reflecting on their achievements, individuals can build a robust, inspiring, and motivating narrative of their artistic journey that not only celebrates their unique contributions but also encourages a deeper exploration of their creativity and artistic identity. This ongoing practice not only counters pervasive self-doubt but also cultivates a genuine sense of belonging within the creative community. It acts as a reminder that individuals are not alone in their struggles, and that their contributions are not only valid but also deserving of recognition and appreciation from their peers and fellow artists. Through this continuous cycle of acknowledgment and reflection, creatives can reinforce their sense of self, celebrate their unique paths, and embrace the intricate journey of their creative lives with renewed vigor, clarity, and confidence. This ultimately leads to a more fulfilling, enriched, and dynamic artistic experience, encouraging continuous growth and exploration in their craft while establishing a strong and resilient foundation for future creative endeavors that will propel them forward in their artistic journeys.

Shifting Focus from External Validation

In the journey of creative expression, countless individuals grapple with a profound and often deep-seated need for external validation. This reliance on external approval can create a debilitating cycle of self-doubt and insecurity, particularly among artists and creators who pour their hearts and souls into their work. Shifting focus from seeking validation from others to cultivating internal confidence is not just beneficial; it is absolutely essential for overcoming the pervasive feelings associated with imposter syndrome that often plague creative minds. By redirecting attention from external sources of affirmation to the more profound and meaningful internal sources of self-worth, artists can reclaim their creative power and pursue their passions with renewed authenticity and vigor. This transition leads to a more profound and enduring sense of fulfillment in their work, allowing them to explore their creativity without the weight of external judgment hanging over them and restricting their true potential. Understanding the underlying reasons behind the dependence on external validation is crucial for any creative individual striving for growth and true artistic expression. Many people have been conditioned from an early age to seek praise and acknowledgment from others, often feeling that their worth is inextricably tied to the approval of peers, mentors, or audiences. This societal pressure can lead to a deeply ingrained belief that one's value is entirely contingent upon the opinions of others, which can fluctuate and vary widely from one person to another, leaving individuals in a constant state of uncertainty. Recognizing and acknowledging this pattern is the first vital step toward breaking free from it and reclaiming one's creative autonomy. Artists must come to realize that their value is intrinsic and not defined by outside opinions, which can often be subjective and shift with circumstances and trends. This crucial realization empowers them to navigate their creative journeys with newfound clarity and confidence, enabling them to express themselves more freely and authentically, which is essential for their development. To foster a healthier and more constructive relationship with oneself, artists can adopt a variety of practices that significantly reinforce self-acceptance and self-compassion. Techniques such as journaling, meditation, and mindfulness can prove invaluable in helping individuals recognize and challenge the negative self-talk that often undermines their confidence and creativity. By diligently documenting accomplishments, regardless of how small they may seem, and reflecting on personal growth over time, creators can build a more robust and resilient sense of self that can withstand external pressures and influences. These practices encourage individuals to celebrate their unique journeys and contributions, shifting the focus away from harmful comparisons and unhealthy competition with others that can stifle originality and self-expression. Furthermore, engaging in creative exercises that highlight personal strengths can enhance self-esteem and self-worth even further, allowing artists to truly appreciate their individual talents and perspectives. This not only fosters a deeper connection to their creative processes but also brings about a profound joy in the act of creating itself. Creating a supportive and nurturing environment is also vital in this transformative process of overcoming the reliance on external validation. Surrounding oneself with like-minded individuals who genuinely value authenticity and creativity can significantly bolster confidence and self-esteem. Engaging in communities that prioritize artistic expression over critique enables artists to share their work without the paralyzing fear of judgment that often stifles creativity and innovation. This sense of camaraderie can provide an invaluable feeling of belonging and reassurance, creating a safe space where creativity can thrive without the oppressive pressure of external validation looming overhead. As artists share their experiences and challenges, they foster an atmosphere of mutual support and encouragement, reinforcing the idea that they are not alone in their struggles and that their unique perspectives and contributions are genuinely valued and appreciated. This collective reinforcement not only enhances individual growth but also enriches the overall creative spirit within the community. Ultimately, the journey toward shifting the focus from external validation to internal authenticity requires ongoing effort, unwavering commitment, and deep self-awareness. Artists must consistently practice self-reflection and surround themselves with positive influences that uplift rather than diminish their spirits. Embracing one's unique creative identity and recognizing that the act of creating is intrinsically valuable can lead to a more fulfilling and enriching artistic experience. By courageously unmasking their fears and insecurities, individuals can fully embrace their roles as creators and contribute their unique voices to the world, free from the constraints and pressures of seeking external approval. This profound shift not only enhances personal growth and self-discovery but also enriches the broader artistic community. It creates a more vibrant and diverse landscape for creativity and expression that benefits everyone involved. Through this transformative journey, artists can cultivate a deeper understanding of their craft, resulting in works that resonate not only with themselves but also with their audience. This, in turn, fosters a rich tapestry of creative expression that uplifts and inspires all, creating an enduring legacy of artistic endeavor and innovation.

Chapter 8: Long-Term Strategies for Success

Continuous Learning and Development

Continuous learning and development are not merely essential; they are fundamentally indispensable components in the journey of any artist. This assertion gains even greater significance for those who grapple with the pervasive and often overwhelming feelings associated with imposter syndrome, a condition that can undermine an artist's confidence and sense of worth. This ongoing, dynamic process serves as a crucial aid for individuals in building their skills, broadening their creative horizons, and ultimately fostering a deep-rooted sense of confidence in their abilities, which is vital for sustaining a fulfilling artistic career. By actively engaging in continuous learning, artists can gain profound insights into their craft that not only enhance their technical skills but also lead to significant contributions to their personal growth and artistic evolution. This growth becomes particularly vital in effectively combating the debilitating feelings of inadequacy that frequently accompany imposter syndrome. It empowers artists to navigate their creative journeys with greater assurance, a more robust sense of self, and an unwavering belief in their unique artistic voice. This profound belief is essential in empowering them to express their individuality, creative vision, and personal experiences without hesitation or fear of judgment, ultimately allowing them to embrace their artistic identity more fully and authentically. By fostering this sense of confidence, artists can explore new avenues of creativity and innovation, enriching both their work and the broader artistic community. One highly effective approach to continuous learning is the pursuit of formal education or structured training, which holds immense value for both emerging and established artists. Engaging in workshops, courses, and seminars provides well-organized environments where artists can develop their skills and explore new techniques in depth, fostering an atmosphere of creativity and growth. Such educational settings not only facilitate invaluable feedback from instructors and peers but also enable individuals to pinpoint specific areas for improvement, creating pathways for targeted skill enhancement. The vibrant exchange of ideas in these collaborative environments nurtures a sense of community that effectively counteracts the isolation that many artists experience in their solitary pursuits. This connection can serve as a powerful reminder that others share similar struggles and challenges, creating a supportive network that fosters personal and artistic growth, while reinforcing the notion that collaboration can lead to innovative breakthroughs and shared success, ultimately enriching the artistic community as a whole. In addition to formal education, self-directed learning plays a significant role in an artist's ongoing development and evolution. This approach can encompass a variety of activities, including reading insightful and thought-provoking books, watching informative tutorials, or exploring a diverse range of online resources that delve into specific techniques or artistic concepts. The inherent flexibility of self-directed learning empowers artists to tailor their educational experiences to their unique interests and needs, making it a highly personalized and profoundly meaningful journey. Engaging with a wide array of information sources can spark new ideas and innovative approaches, serving as a catalyst for creativity and artistic expression. This exploration not only bolsters technical prowess but also reinforces the empowering notion that learning is a lifelong journey filled with endless opportunities for growth, discovery, and the expansion of one's creative repertoire, allowing artists to continuously evolve and redefine their artistic identities. Mentorship stands out as an essential and invaluable aspect of continuous learning that should never be underestimated or overlooked. Establishing meaningful and deep relationships with more experienced artists provides essential guidance and unwavering support throughout the often tumultuous and sometimes unpredictable creative journey. Mentors offer valuable insights into navigating the myriad challenges of the creative field, sharing their own experiences with the complexities of imposter syndrome, and providing much-needed encouragement during difficult and uncertain times. This nurturing and supportive relationship can help demystify the creative process while normalizing the struggles that many artists inevitably face along the way. By learning from those who have successfully navigated similar challenges, individuals can find reassurance and strength in their own journeys, ultimately reducing feelings of self-doubt and fostering resilience in the face of adversity. This resilience is crucial for achieving long-term growth and satisfaction in their artistic careers, empowering them to embrace their unique paths with confidence and determination. They can approach their creative endeavors knowing that they are not alone in their struggles and challenges. Ultimately, continuous learning and personal development empower artists to fully embrace their identities and inherent talents in profoundly transformative ways. By committing to ongoing education, actively seeking mentorship, and engaging deeply with their creative communities, artists can effectively counteract the negative effects of imposter syndrome that often plague them. This proactive and intentional approach not only enhances artistic skills but also cultivates a positive mindset that celebrates growth, resilience, and unwavering self-acceptance. As artists navigate their complex creative pursuits, they can find profound strength in the knowledge that every step taken toward learning is a vital step away from self-doubt and toward a more profound sense of self-acceptance, fulfillment, and artistic empowerment in their creative endeavors. Such empowerment encourages them to continuously explore their artistic boundaries and potential. This steadfast commitment to personal and professional growth ensures that artists remain vibrant contributors to their artistic communities while continuously evolving and refining their unique voices. They enrich both their lives and the lives of those around them in meaningful and lasting ways. This journey of self-discovery and creative exploration ultimately fosters a deeper connection to their art and those who appreciate it, creating an enriching cycle of growth and support within the broader community that benefits everyone involved.

Staying Resilient in the Face of Challenges

Resilience stands as an immensely vital quality for anyone navigating the often-tumultuous waters of creative endeavors, and its importance truly cannot be overstated. When confronted with a multitude of challenges—whether they arise from self-doubt, external criticism, or the inevitable sting of failure—maintaining a resilient mindset can profoundly impact the trajectory of an artist's career, frequently determining their capacity to thrive in an unpredictable and often chaotic environment. Resilience empowers individuals to recover from setbacks, glean invaluable lessons from their experiences, and persist in pursuing their passions, even in the face of adversity that may seem overwhelming and insurmountable. It is crucial to recognize that challenges are not only unavoidable but also integral to the very essence of the creative process. Embracing this perspective can fundamentally assist artists in viewing obstacles as opportunities for growth and development rather than insurmountable barriers that hinder their progress. This crucial shift in mindset transforms the artist's journey into one characterized by ongoing learning and adaptation, facilitating personal and professional evolution that enriches their artistic expression and overall creative output. One highly effective technique for nurturing resilience is the practice of self-compassion, which plays a fundamental role in an artist's journey toward fulfillment and self-discovery. Instead of resorting to harsh self-criticism that can be profoundly detrimental to their creative spirit and motivation, artists can greatly benefit from treating themselves with kindness, understanding, and patience during challenging periods. This compassionate approach cultivates a healthier self-image and encourages individuals to acknowledge their feelings without judgment or harshness, allowing them to embrace their vulnerabilities and imperfections. By recognizing that everyone encounters challenges and that imperfection is an inherent aspect of the human experience, artists can alleviate some of the pressure they impose on themselves, fostering a more forgiving internal dialogue. This empowering mindset not only enhances emotional well-being but also fosters persistence and determination in the face of adversity. Practicing self-compassion enables artists to establish a nurturing inner dialogue that reinforces their resilience and fortitude, empowering them to navigate the inevitable highs and lows of their creative pursuits with greater ease, confidence, and grace, ultimately enriching their artistic journey. Another crucial strategy for fostering resilience is to cultivate a supportive network of fellow creatives, which can be transformative and immensely beneficial. Engaging with other artists can impart a profound sense of camaraderie and validation, which is particularly vital for those wrestling with feelings of inadequacy and imposter syndrome that often accompany the intricate and demanding creative process. Sharing experiences, challenges, and even triumphs with others can help individuals realize they are not alone in their struggles, creating a comforting sense of belonging that is essential for emotional sustenance and encouragement. This collective support acts as a powerful reminder that creativity is often a shared journey, where collaboration can yield innovative solutions and encouragement in times of need. Building and nurturing such relationships can be instrumental in fostering resilience, as they provide both emotional support and practical guidance during trying times. A strong community not only amplifies motivation but also creates a safe space for artists to express themselves freely, ultimately enhancing their creative output and broadening their horizons, allowing them to explore new ideas and artistic avenues with confidence, enthusiasm, and a renewed sense of purpose Setting realistic and achievable goals is also essential in sustaining resilience amid the challenges that artists frequently encounter. Artists often experience pressure to achieve perfection, which can lead to feelings of inadequacy and frustration when they fall short of those lofty expectations. By establishing achievable, incremental goals, individuals can create a sense of accomplishment that fortifies their confidence and self-worth. Celebrating small victories along the way reinforces the understanding that progress is a journey, not merely a destination. This approach helps to mitigate feelings of failure and encourages artists to persist, even when the path ahead appears daunting and uncertain. By breaking larger ambitions into manageable steps, artists can maintain momentum and focus, sustaining their creative passion over the long haul, and ensuring their artistic vision remains vibrant and alive. Finally, cultivating a growth mindset is absolutely crucial to remaining resilient throughout the multifaceted and often unpredictable creative journey that every artist embarks upon. This mindset encourages individuals to view challenges not merely as obstacles but as invaluable opportunities for learning and personal growth, transforming them into powerful catalysts rather than threats to their abilities and self-esteem. Embracing failure as a natural, and frequently necessary, part of the intricate creative process empowers artists to experiment freely, take risks, and explore new avenues without the paralyzing fear of being judged or criticized by others. By actively reframing setbacks as essential stepping stones to improvement, individuals can sustain their motivation and unwavering commitment to their craft, even in the face of adversity and uncertainty. Resilience, therefore, evolves from being merely a reactive response to challenges into a proactive approach that empowers artists to navigate their creative journeys with renewed confidence, determination, and a profound sense of purpose that fuels their artistic expression in meaningful and impactful ways. Adopting this perspective ultimately nurtures an enduring passion for creativity, enabling artists not only to survive but also to thrive in an ever-evolving landscape brimming with possibilities and abundant opportunities for innovation, exploration, and deep self-discovery. Embracing this broader vision of resilience and growth can significantly enhance the artistic experience, allowing individuals to fully engage with their creative potential and express themselves more authentically and powerfully. This transformation in perspective not only enriches the individual artist's journey but also contributes to a vibrant and dynamic creative community, fostering collaboration and inspiration among peers, thus creating an environment where creativity can flourish. As artists share their experiences and insights, they not only inspire one another but also cultivate a sense of belonging and support that is vital for personal and collective growth in the arts. In this way, the artistic journey becomes not just a solitary pursuit but a shared adventure that celebrates the diversity of expression and the richness of human experience.

Integrating Strategies into Daily Practice

Integrating effective strategies to combat imposter syndrome into daily practice is not merely beneficial; it is absolutely essential for cultivating a healthy and resilient mindset in creative fields. The first step in this transformative journey involves recognizing that imposter syndrome is not an isolated experience but rather a common challenge faced by countless artists, writers, musicians, and other creatives across various disciplines. Acknowledging that numerous individuals share these feelings can be incredibly liberating and empowering. By normalizing these complex emotions, individuals can begin to dismantle the overwhelming power that self-doubt holds over them. Embracing the reality that self-doubt and feelings of inadequacy are intrinsic parts of the creative journey allows artists to approach their work with renewed confidence, authenticity, and a deep sense of purpose, ultimately enriching their creative expression and fueling their artistic drive. One effective strategy for integrating these techniques into daily life is to establish a consistent and intentional routine that includes dedicated self-reflection. Setting aside time each day to evaluate personal achievements, regardless of how small or seemingly insignificant they may appear, can significantly help shift focus away from perceived shortcomings toward recognized strengths and accomplishments. Journaling emerges as a powerful and impactful tool in this context; it provides a safe and private space to articulate thoughts and feelings, allowing creatives to process their emotions in a constructive and meaningful manner. This practice not only offers valuable insights into patterns of self-doubt but also cultivates a habit of celebrating progress and recognizing the journey itself. It reinforces the notion that growth is an ongoing and dynamic process, not merely a destination to be reached. Furthermore, reflecting on personal narratives can enhance self-awareness, enabling creatives to identify triggers of self-doubt and develop effective strategies to navigate them. This ultimately leads to a more fulfilling and enriching creative journey, where individuals feel better equipped to handle challenges as they arise, fostering resilience and adaptability in their artistic pursuits. In addition to self-reflection, creating a supportive community is absolutely vital for overcoming feelings of inadequacy and persistent self-doubt that many creatives face. Engaging with peers in various creative fields can provide much-needed reassurance and validation that counteracts those pervasive feelings of self-doubt. Regularly participating in group workshops, networking events, or online forums can facilitate the sharing of experiences and strategies for overcoming imposter syndrome collaboratively. By exchanging stories, insights, and coping strategies, individuals can come to a powerful realization that they are not alone in their struggles, which fosters a profound sense of belonging and collective strength among creatives. This communal approach not only encourages artists to uplift one another but also creates an environment where creativity can truly flourish without the heavy burden of self-doubt weighing them down. Additionally, forming connections with mentors or role models can provide invaluable guidance and inspiration, further enriching the creative process and reinforcing the belief that everyone grapples with similar challenges and experiences along their artistic journeys. This creates a more supportive ecosystem for all individuals involved in creative pursuits, enhancing the overall experience of artistic expression and collaboration. Another important strategy is to actively challenge negative self-talk on a daily basis, which can significantly enhance one's mindset and overall creative output. Individuals should diligently strive to become more aware of their internal dialogue, consciously replacing detrimental thoughts with positive affirmations and constructive feedback. This transformative process demands diligent and consistent practice but can be effectively woven into daily routines with strong commitment and dedication. For instance, creating a comprehensive list of affirmations or positive statements about one's work, skills, and talents can serve as a powerful daily reminder of one's worth and capabilities, reinforcing the belief in one's potential. By consistently countering negative narratives with empowering thoughts, creatives can gradually retrain their minds to focus on their unique talents and contributions, thereby diminishing the pervasive impact of imposter syndrome over time and reinforcing a healthier self-image. Establishing a habit of verbalizing affirmations in front of a mirror or sharing them with a trusted friend can further enhance this practice, making it even more impactful and reinforcing a positive mindset that cultivates resilience in creative endeavors. Ultimately, this leads to a more confident and fulfilled creative life, where individuals are not only able to acknowledge their worth but also thrive in their artistic pursuits with greater passion, purpose, and a renewed sense of inspiration that invigorates their work, leading to innovative ideas and breakthroughs that can transform their approach to creativity. Lastly, it is absolutely crucial and invaluable for growth to wholeheartedly embrace failure as a natural and inevitable component of the creative process. By reframing setbacks and disappointments as valuable learning opportunities, artists can cultivate resilience and adaptability within their practices. This perspective allows for a richer and more fulfilling creative experience that can truly enrich one's artistic journey. Engaging in daily practices such as setting realistic and achievable goals, while also allowing ample room for experimentation and exploration, can significantly alleviate the paralyzing fear of failure that often accompanies the creative journey. Understanding that every artist has faced rejection or produced work that did not meet their expectations can truly liberate individuals from the confines of perfectionism that can stifle creativity and innovation. This understanding fosters a more compassionate and forgiving view of oneself throughout the creative process, promoting overall well-being. By incorporating these thoughtful strategies into their daily lives and nurturing an attitude of curiosity and openness, creatives can effectively combat the pervasive feelings of imposter syndrome that may arise. This proactive approach not only nurtures a more positive, enriching, and productive relationship with their artistic endeavors and overall creative expression but also enhances their confidence and self-awareness. Ultimately, it leads to a deeper engagement with their craft, a more fulfilling creative journey, and a stronger connection to their artistic identity. This connection can not only inspire themselves but also motivate and uplift others in the creative community, creating a shared environment of encouragement and innovation. Through this collective experience, artists can thrive, pushing the boundaries of their creativity even further while fostering a vibrant and supportive community that uplifts everyone involved.

Chapter 9: Case Studies and Real-Life Examples

Artists Who Conquered Imposter Syndrome

Imposter syndrome is a pervasive and often debilitating feeling of self-doubt that countless artists encounter throughout their careers, leading them to incessantly question their abilities, skills, and accomplishments. This psychological hurdle, which has affected innumerable artists throughout history, can create significant barriers to personal and professional growth. Yet, despite these challenges, many artists have managed to rise above their insecurities, making remarkable contributions to their respective fields. By examining the journeys and stories of these individuals, contemporary artists can gain invaluable insights and practical techniques to successfully navigate similar emotional challenges. Delving into the experiences of these notable figures reveals effective strategies that can assist anyone engaged in creative pursuits in combating the pervasive feelings associated with imposter syndrome. This exploration ultimately fosters resilience, self-acceptance, and a renewed sense of purpose and determination that can propel their artistic endeavors forward in meaningful ways. One such inspiring artist is Maya Angelou, whose extraordinary literary talent and powerful voice have inspired countless generations and left an indelible mark on the realms of literature and activism. Despite receiving a plethora of accolades, awards, and honors throughout her life, Angelou often grappled with the nagging feeling that she was a fraud, firmly convinced that her success stemmed merely from luck rather than being a true reflection of her substantial talent and hard work. To manage these debilitating feelings of inadequacy, she adopted a simple yet highly effective technique: she made it a priority to recognize and acknowledge her achievements while actively reframing her mindset to focus on her strengths and positive attributes. By appreciating the hard work, determination, and persistence that paved the way for her numerous successes, she was able to combat her self-doubt and fully embrace her identity as a writer and poet. This practice of self-reflection serves as a powerful tool for artists today, encouraging them to recognize their own worth and contributions while fostering a deeper appreciation for their unique talents and the significance of the effort that goes into their creative processes. Another prominent figure in the arts is Vincent van Gogh, whose tumultuous and often tragic life was characterized by extraordinary creativity, passion, and deep-seated self-doubt that frequently plagued him. Van Gogh often grappled with feelings of inadequacy, firmly convinced that his work would never receive the appreciation and acknowledgment it so richly deserved. To counter these pervasive negative thoughts, he chose to immerse himself in his art, focusing intently on the act of creation itself rather than seeking external validation or approval from others. This approach underscores the importance of discovering fulfillment within the creative process, emphasizing that true satisfaction arises from personal expression and the joy of creation rather than from external accolades or recognition. By prioritizing personal passion and creativity over perceived success, contemporary artists can learn to silence their inner critics, cultivate a healthier and more positive relationship with their work, and ultimately foster a sense of joy and fulfillment in their creative endeavors. This allows their artistic voices to flourish uninhibited and freely, enabling them to contribute authentically to the vibrant tapestry of the art world, enriching it with their unique perspectives and experiences Frida Kahlo's story further exemplifies the struggle against imposter syndrome, illustrating the complexities of an artist's emotional landscape and the burdens they may carry. Despite her distinctive artistic style and profound impact on the art world, Kahlo often felt unworthy of the acclaim and recognition she received from both critics and audiences alike. She coped with her feelings of inadequacy by embracing vulnerability and authenticity in her creative expression, which allowed her to connect deeply with her audience on a personal level. By painting her pain and personal experiences, she transformed her struggles into powerful artistic statements that resonated profoundly with many, creating a lasting legacy that continues to inspire new generations of artists. This approach emphasizes the significance of vulnerability in creative expression, illustrating how embracing one's true self can lead to extraordinary artistic breakthroughs and personal growth. Artists today can greatly benefit from allowing their unique experiences to shape their work, fostering a profound sense of connection that can help alleviate feelings of impostorism and self-doubt while enhancing their creative expression, ultimately leading to a more fulfilling and enriching artistic journey filled with passion and purpose. Lastly, the inspiring journey of actor and filmmaker Viola Davis provides an even richer source of motivation for those grappling with feelings of inadequacy in their artistic pursuits. Davis, who has garnered remarkable success and widespread recognition throughout her illustrious career, has been refreshingly candid about her own struggles with self-doubt and persistent feelings of being an imposter in the highly competitive and often unforgiving realm of Hollywood. She emphasizes the critical importance of community, connection, and support in overcoming the challenging emotions that many artists encounter on their paths. Engaging meaningfully with fellow artists, sharing personal experiences, and actively seeking mentorship can create a powerful sense of belonging that significantly diminishes feelings of isolation and self-doubt. By building a supportive network of peers and mentors, artists can continually remind themselves that they are not alone in their struggles and that their experiences are entirely valid and deserving of acknowledgment. This profound sense of solidarity ultimately empowers them to embrace their creative journeys with renewed confidence, a clear sense of purpose, and a deeper understanding of their own artistic value. Such an environment fosters a culture where creativity can truly flourish, allowing artists to thrive, explore their unique expressions, and convey their stories without fear of judgment or inadequacy. In this nurturing atmosphere, they can push boundaries, take risks, and fully realize their potential as creators, enriching the artistic landscape for everyone involved. Moreover, the shared experiences and collective wisdom that arise from these connections can lead to collaborative projects that further enhance their artistic endeavors, encouraging a vibrant exchange of ideas and inspiration that benefits not just the individual artist but the broader community as well. In this way, the journey towards overcoming self-doubt becomes not only a personal triumph but also a shared adventure that uplifts and elevates the entire artistic community.

Interviews with Creative Professionals

Interviews with a wide array of creative professionals reveal an intricate and rich tapestry of diverse experiences that highlight the pervasive nature of imposter syndrome across numerous artistic disciplines. These enlightening conversations provide invaluable insights into how artists, writers, designers, and other creatives navigate the complexities of self-doubt, alongside the often-overwhelming feelings of inadequacy that can arise and evolve throughout their careers. By sharing their personal stories candidly, these professionals not only validate the struggles faced by many on a daily basis but also offer practical strategies for overcoming the paralyzing effects of imposter syndrome, which can significantly hinder both their artistic expression and professional growth over time. Numerous creatives consistently report that imposter syndrome manifests during pivotal moments in their careers, events that often define their creative paths. These can include the launch of an exciting new project, the receipt of a prestigious award, or even during high-stakes presentations to influential audiences. In their interviews, they describe intense feelings of being "found out" or feeling profoundly unworthy of their hard-earned achievements, experiences that can be deeply overwhelming and incredibly challenging to manage. For instance, a designer may feel that their current success is merely a product of luck or external validation rather than a true reflection of their own talent, creativity, and relentless hard work. Such perceptions can lead to a damaging cycle of self-doubt that stifles and inhibits their creative process, making it difficult for them to express their true artistic vision. These poignant revelations underscore the vital importance of recognizing that such feelings are not only common but also do not diminish one's inherent abilities or accomplishments. Furthermore, these experiences are often shared among peers who face similar challenges and insecurities, creating a profound sense of camaraderie in the experience of self-doubt that can alleviate some of the burdens associated with it, fostering a supportive community among those who understand these struggles. To effectively combat these pervasive feelings of inadequacy, many professionals emphasize the indispensable value of community and support networks in their lives. Interviewees frequently mention the invaluable role of mentors, supportive peers, and even online forums where they can share their experiences, seek advice, and offer encouragement to one another in times of need. Building authentic connections with others in the creative field not only fosters a deep sense of belonging but also provides crucial reassurance that their feelings of self-doubt are shared by others who are facing comparable challenges and adversities. This nurturing and supportive environment can help demystify the experience of imposter syndrome, making it significantly easier for individuals to confront and challenge their negative beliefs about themselves and the true value of their work. Ultimately, this transformative process reshapes their inner dialogue and fosters a healthier mindset that can lead to greater artistic fulfillment and personal satisfaction, allowing them to thrive, flourish, and excel in their respective fields while overcoming the hurdles posed by self-doubt, and enabling them to embrace their creative identities with renewed confidence and vigor. Another widely recognized and effective strategy identified through these insightful interviews is the practice of self-reflection and positive affirmation. Creatives often engage in reflective practices, such as journaling, meditation, or even artistic expression, to process their thoughts and emotions, allowing them to gain clarity on their complex feelings and experiences. They highlight the importance of recognizing and celebrating their achievements, no matter how small or seemingly insignificant, as a powerful means of countering self-doubt and reinforcing their sense of self-worth. By intentionally focusing on their strengths, talents, and successes, these professionals can cultivate a more positive self-image and reinforce their identity as competent and deserving artists within their respective fields and communities. This practice ultimately fosters resilience and a greater sense of purpose, enhancing their long-term artistic journeys and contributing significantly to their overall well-being, enabling them to pursue their passions with renewed vigor and confidence. Finally, many interviewees passionately advocate for embracing vulnerability as a profound strength rather than a weakness. By openly discussing their personal struggles with imposter syndrome, creatives can not only alleviate their own burdens of self-doubt but also inspire and empower others to confront their own fears and uncertainties. This culture of openness fosters authenticity within creative circles, encouraging individuals to be honest about their challenges and seek help when needed. Ultimately, these interviews illustrate that overcoming the debilitating effects of imposter syndrome is not a solitary journey but rather a communal effort, where sharing experiences and effective strategies can empower all creatives to embrace their true potential. This collaborative spirit enables them to build resilience and thrive in their artistic endeavors and professional pursuits. It fosters a more supportive and understanding creative community that values collaboration, shared growth, and collective success, reinforcing the idea that together, individuals can achieve greater heights than they ever could alone. In addition to these methods, it is essential to recognize that the process of healing from self-doubt and imposter syndrome is ongoing, requiring continuous effort, resilience, and a deep commitment to personal growth. Many interviewees stress the importance of regular check-ins with themselves and their support networks, ensuring that they remain connected and accountable in their personal and professional development. By consistently engaging with their communities and dedicating time to self-reflection, creatives can navigate the ups and downs of their journeys with greater ease and confidence, transforming moments of doubt into invaluable opportunities for self-discovery and empowerment. Through this lens, the creative process evolves into not just a pursuit of excellence but also a profound journey of self-acceptance, where artists can fully embrace their unique voices and contributions to the world. This atmosphere encourages a rich tapestry of perspectives that enhances the creative landscape for everyone involved, cultivating a nurturing environment where creativity can flourish and individuals feel genuinely valued for their authentic selves. In this dynamic setting, the synergy among creatives enhances their collective ability to innovate and inspire, reinforcing the notion that mutual support and understanding are crucial components of artistic expression and success.

Lessons Learned from Their Journeys

The experiences of artists and creative professionals often intersect profoundly with the feelings of self-doubt and inadequacy that define imposter syndrome. Many individuals in the creative sphere have courageously shared their diverse journeys, illustrating that the road to overcoming these pervasive feelings is rarely linear or straightforward. Each unique personal story offers valuable lessons that serve as essential guideposts for others navigating similar struggles in their own creative lives. By understanding and reflecting on these lessons, aspiring creatives can illuminate their paths, equipping themselves with the tools and insights necessary to cultivate a deeper sense of confidence in their artistic abilities and endeavors. Ultimately, this extensive process allows them to embrace their true potential and explore new horizons in their work, paving the way for innovative expressions and groundbreaking discoveries that can redefine their artistic identities. One of the most significant lessons learned throughout these experiences is the critical importance of embracing vulnerability. Many artists initially felt an overwhelming compulsion to present a facade of unwavering confidence, fueled by a deep-seated fear of judgment from peers and audiences alike. However, those who achieved genuine success came to recognize that their willingness to show vulnerability enabled them to connect more authentically with others, fostering deeper and more meaningful relationships that enriched their artistic journeys. By sharing their insecurities and challenges, they not only cultivated empathy among their peers but also created a supportive environment where open dialogue about the realities of imposter syndrome became both possible and encouraged. This contributed to a richer community experience, allowing individuals to feel seen, heard, and understood in their struggles. This powerful lesson underscores the notion that vulnerability can serve as a formidable strength in the creative process, rather than as a debilitating weakness that hinders progress and expression. It reveals that true connections blossom when individuals allow their authentic selves to shine through their work, ultimately leading to a more enriching and fulfilling artistic journey filled with growth, exploration, and profound insights. Another essential insight revolves around the necessity of mentorship and community support. Many creatives discovered that actively seeking guidance from more experienced individuals provided them with both reassurance and invaluable perspective on their journeys. Mentorship relationships often highlighted shared experiences of self-doubt, effectively helping to demystify the narrative of the solitary genius and the myth surrounding the individual artist. Creating or joining supportive communities, where individuals can openly share their struggles and triumphs, fosters a profound sense of belonging and validation that is crucial for personal and professional growth. These meaningful connections serve as vital reminders for artists that they are not alone in their feelings of inadequacy and that collaboration can lead to substantial personal growth and artistic development. Ultimately, this significantly enhances their creative journeys, providing the encouragement and motivation needed to venture into new territories of artistic exploration and expression. The strength found in unity and shared experiences becomes a beacon of hope for those feeling isolated in their struggles, encouraging them to open up, seek support, and nurture their artistic ambitions when needed, ultimately enriching their creative trajectories in ways they might never have imagined. Additionally, the practice of self-compassion emerged as an essential lesson for many artists navigating the often unpredictable and sometimes chaotic twists and turns of their creative journeys. Rather than succumbing to harsh self-criticism and negative inner dialogue that can easily derail progress and diminish motivation, successful creatives learned to treat themselves with kindness, empathy, and understanding, particularly during moments of failure or perceived inadequacy. This transformative shift in mindset allowed them to view setbacks not merely as obstacles to overcome but as invaluable opportunities for growth and learning, rather than as definitive judgments of their worth and capabilities as artists. By cultivating self-compassion, individuals can create a more nurturing and supportive internal dialogue that actively encourages risk-taking and exploration, both of which are essential components of the creative process and artistic expression. This internal kindness fosters resilience, enabling artists to rebound from challenges with renewed vigor, creativity, and determination, ultimately enriching their artistic expression and enhancing their overall journey in the vast, multifaceted, and often complex creative world. Moreover, the power of continuous learning and experimentation proved to be profoundly transformative for many artists, encouraging them to embrace change and adaptability in their practices. Numerous creatives realized that granting themselves the freedom to explore new techniques, ideas, and mediums without the crushing pressure of perfectionism significantly alleviated the heavy weight of imposter syndrome that so often stifles authentic creative expression. This open and exploratory approach not only expanded their skill sets dramatically but also rekindled their passion for their craft and deepened their engagement with the nuances of creative expression. Embracing the idea that mastery is a journey rather than a fixed destination can empower creatives to pursue their artistic endeavors with renewed enthusiasm, curiosity, and a sense of adventure that invigorates their work and fuels their imagination. These valuable lessons, drawn from the journeys of those who have faced and ultimately conquered imposter syndrome, provide a comprehensive and insightful roadmap for others striving to reclaim their voices and confidence in the ever-evolving, dynamic creative landscape. This encourages them to embrace their unique paths with courage, resilience, and an unwavering belief in their potential, serving as a powerful reminder that the journey itself is just as important as the destination, filled with rich experiences that shape their artistic identity and personal growth along the way. By integrating these insights into their creative lives, artists can not only enhance their individual practices but also contribute to a more vibrant and supportive artistic community, where collaboration and shared experiences further enrich the creative process.

Chapter 10: Moving Forward

Creating Your Personal Action Plan

Creating a personal action plan is not only an essential but also a deeply transformative step in addressing and ultimately overcoming the pervasive feelings associated with imposter syndrome. This aspect is particularly crucial in creative fields, where self-doubt can often feel overwhelmingly present, significantly affecting artists in numerous ways. This action plan serves as a comprehensive and detailed roadmap, outlining specific, actionable steps tailored to your unique experiences, challenges, and aspirations as an artist or creative individual. To embark on this empowering journey, it is vital first to identify your specific triggers for imposter feelings. Take dedicated time to reflect deeply on the various situations and contexts that lead you to feel inadequate or where self-doubt begins to creep in, whether in the form of criticism, comparison, or even personal setbacks. By thoroughly recognizing these triggers, you empower yourself to formulate effective strategies designed specifically to combat them, thereby significantly reducing their negative impact on your creative work and overall well-being. Next, set clear and achievable goals that align harmoniously with your creative aspirations and vision, ensuring that they resonate deeply with your personal motivations and desires. These goals should be specific, measurable, attainable, relevant, and timely, often referred to as SMART goals. Instead of setting a vague goal like "become a better artist," you might establish a more precise and concrete goal, such as committing to complete a certain number of artwork pieces within a specific timeframe. For example, aim to finish five paintings in the next two months, allowing yourself the opportunity to hone your skills while also exploring new techniques and ideas in various styles. This heightened clarity not only serves to motivate you but also provides a strong sense of direction, making it easier to track your progress and celebrate your achievements along the way, no matter how minor they may seem. This practice fosters an invaluable sense of accomplishment that boosts your confidence and reinforces your commitment to your artistic journey, enabling you to cultivate a more profound connection to your work and a richer appreciation for your creative process. Incorporating regular self-reflection into your action plan can significantly enhance your ability to combat the effects of imposter syndrome while nurturing your creative spirit in profound and meaningful ways. Schedule dedicated time on a weekly or monthly basis to thoroughly assess your accomplishments and evaluate your feelings about your creative journey. During these reflections, focus on actively acknowledging your successes and milestones, no matter how small they may appear at first glance. This consistent practice helps to reinforce a positive self-image over time and gradually diminishes the power of the negative thoughts and feelings that often accompany imposter syndrome. This reflective process enables you to build resilience against self-doubt and cultivate a healthier mindset geared toward growth, enhancing your ability to face challenges head-on with renewed vigor, determination, and a strong sense of purpose. In addition to the essential steps outlined, it is crucial to emphasize the significance of surrounding yourself with a nurturing and supportive community of fellow artists and creatives who truly understand the various struggles associated with imposter syndrome. Actively engaging with peers who can offer genuine encouragement, valuable feedback, and constructive criticism within a safe and nurturing environment can greatly enhance your experience. By sharing your experiences and challenges with others, you can cultivate a profound sense of camaraderie, which serves as a vital reassurance that you are not alone in your feelings of self-doubt. This collective support acts as a powerful reminder of your inherent capabilities and reinforces your unwavering commitment to your artistic journey. By intentionally fostering connections with like-minded individuals, you not only create an additional layer of accountability but also establish a rich source of motivation that can propel you further toward your goals and creative aspirations. Moreover, another critical aspect of your personal action plan should include the conscious and deliberate building of a robust support system that continuously uplifts and inspires you throughout your creative journey. Surrounding yourself with other creatives who genuinely understand and empathize with your struggles can provide both encouragement and accountability as you navigate your artistic path. Consider actively seeking out workshops, online forums, or local art groups where you can share your experiences, gain valuable insights from others who are facing similar challenges, and even collaborate on projects that can invigorate your creativity and spark fresh ideas. Engaging in open discussions about imposter syndrome not only serves to normalize these feelings but also perpetually reminds you that you are not alone on this journey. This fosters a profound sense of community, connection, and understanding that can be incredibly reassuring and beneficial for your artistic growth. Ultimately, this dynamic network can shape a more supportive environment for your creative exploration, making your path as an artist feel increasingly collaborative, enriching, and fulfilling, while also allowing you to cultivate deeper relationships with fellow artists who share your passion and vision. Lastly, it is essential to be prepared to adapt and evolve your action plan as you grow and progress in your creative pursuits. Life is inherently dynamic and ever-changing, and your goals may shift and transform as you encounter new experiences, insights, and perspectives along your journey. Regularly revisiting and updating your action plan ensures that it remains relevant, effective, and responsive to your evolving relationship with imposter syndrome and your artistic ambitions. Embrace this journey fully, recognizing that overcoming imposter syndrome is not merely a one-time achievement but rather a continuous process that requires patience, commitment, and, above all, a profound sense of self-compassion and understanding for yourself as you navigate the complexities and rich tapestry of your creative life. This ongoing journey not only enhances your artistic expression but also reinforces your emotional resilience, preparing you to face future challenges with confidence and grace. This preparation helps you thrive in your creative endeavors while nurturing a deeper appreciation for your unique artistic voice and the myriad nuances that define your individual journey. Adopting this holistic approach to your creative development can yield transformative results, enriching both your art and your personal growth, ultimately leading to a more fulfilling and impactful creative life that resonates deeply with both you and your audience.

Developing a Lifelong Practice of Self-Acceptance

Developing a lifelong practice of self-acceptance is absolutely essential for anyone navigating the often intricate and multifaceted complexities of creative pursuits, particularly for those grappling with the burdens of imposter syndrome. Self-acceptance involves not only recognizing but also wholeheartedly embracing one's true self, which encompasses strengths, weaknesses, and the unique qualities that each individual possesses. This acceptance forms the very foundation upon which artists can build a robust resilience against self-doubt and the persistent fear of being exposed as a fraud. This practice transcends being merely an emotional exercise; it demands a conscious, deliberate effort and a steadfast commitment to nurturing a mindset that prioritizes authenticity over the often unattainable ideal of perfection, which can lead to frustration and disillusionment. One of the initial and most vital steps in cultivating genuine self-acceptance involves actively challenging and confronting the negative self-talk that can plague many individuals. Individuals frequently internalize critical voices that significantly undermine their confidence and creativity, often manifesting as debilitating thoughts that keep them from fully engaging with their artistic endeavors and expressing their true potential. By identifying these negative thoughts and reframing them into more positive and constructive narratives, artists can begin to replace self-criticism with a much-needed sense of compassion and kindness towards themselves. Techniques such as journaling can prove to be particularly beneficial in this transformative process, allowing individuals to articulate their feelings more clearly and reflect deeply on their experiences in ways that promote healing and understanding. Over time, this practice can lead to a more balanced and nuanced perspective that highlights accomplishments while also recognizing the inherent value of learning from failures, which are an integral part of any creative journey. These failures provide essential lessons that contribute to personal and artistic growth, enriching the overall creative experience. Another essential and pivotal aspect of self-acceptance involves setting realistic and attainable expectations for oneself. Many creatives, unfortunately, fall into the common trap of comparing themselves to others, a tendency that inevitably leads to feelings of inadequacy and frustration that can stifle creativity and self-expression. It is crucial to acknowledge that every artist has a unique journey, filled with its own distinct challenges and milestones that shape their work and perspective over time. By focusing on personal growth rather than rigid external benchmarks, individuals can better appreciate their own progress and understand that mastery in any field is a gradual and often nonlinear process, filled with both successes and setbacks. This significant shift in focus can greatly alleviate the pressure that often accompanies creative endeavors, allowing for a more fulfilling and enriching experience that fosters joy and satisfaction in the creative process. Ultimately, this leads to more authentic artistic expression that resonates deeply with both the artist and their audience, creating a meaningful connection that enriches the creative community as a whole. Incorporating mindfulness practices into daily routines can significantly enhance self-acceptance in profound and transformative ways. Mindfulness encourages individuals to remain fully present in each moment, allowing them to observe their thoughts and feelings without judgment or bias. This deliberate awareness creates a valuable space for deeper emotional exploration and understanding, which is essential for personal growth and development. For creatives, this practice can lead to a much richer understanding of their own emotions and the deeper roots of their self-doubt. It shines a light on patterns and behaviors that may have previously gone unnoticed or unexamined, paving the way for a transformative journey toward self-discovery and authenticity. Techniques such as meditation, deep breathing exercises, or even simple mindful walking can create an invaluable environment for self-reflection and appreciation of one's unique creative journey and contributions. Through consistent mindfulness practice, artists learn to accept their experiences and feelings as valid and legitimate, fostering a more compassionate and nurturing relationship with themselves. This nurturing relationship can lead to greater creativity, enhanced productivity, and an overall increase in artistic output, enriching not only their personal lives but also their artistic endeavors in meaningful and significant ways. Furthermore, building a supportive and understanding community can greatly reinforce the ongoing practice of self-acceptance and emotional resilience. Surrounding oneself with fellow creatives who share similar struggles and experiences can create an enriching environment filled with encouragement, support, and mutual understanding. Open discussions about vulnerabilities, failures, and successes help normalize the feelings associated with imposter syndrome and promote a culture of acceptance and support that is vital in creative circles. Engaging in collaborative projects or sharing one's work with others can further enhance this sense of belonging and connection, reminding individuals that they are not alone in their experiences and challenges. Through these meaningful and authentic connections, artists can cultivate a continuous and evolving practice of self-acceptance that not only supports their creative ambitions but also nurtures their personal growth and overall well-being. This sense of community serves as a powerful catalyst for transformation, empowering individuals to embrace their true selves and pursue their passions with renewed vigor and enthusiasm, ultimately enriching their lives and artistic journeys in ways that resonate deeply and lastingly, creating a ripple effect of positive change throughout their creative process and personal lives.

Inspiring Others: Sharing Your Journey

Inspiring others through the sharing of your journey is an incredibly powerful tool for overcoming imposter syndrome, particularly in creative fields where self-doubt can be pervasive and overwhelming. When individuals choose to openly discuss their experiences, including both their struggles with self-doubt and the proactive steps they took to navigate and ultimately overcome these challenges, they provide relatable narratives that resonate deeply with others who may be feeling similarly. This genuine connection fosters a profound sense of community and belonging, allowing fellow creatives to feel understood, validated, and supported in their own experiences and insecurities. Sharing your journey goes beyond merely highlighting successes; it involves a candid acknowledgment of failures, setbacks, and the emotional turmoil that often accompanies creative pursuits. These aspects can be just as important, if not more so, than celebrating achievements, as they create a more holistic understanding of the creative process and enrich the discourse around creativity and its inherent challenges. One particularly effective method of sharing your journey is through engaging storytelling that captivates and inspires. By recounting specific moments that led to feelings of inadequacy or fear, you can vividly illustrate the universal nature of these experiences, making them more relatable and accessible. For instance, describing a pivotal moment when you almost gave up on a project due to overwhelming self-doubt can create a compelling narrative that resonates with others grappling with similar feelings of uncertainty and hesitation. This narrative can find expression through various platforms, such as social media, personal blogs, podcasts, or public speaking engagements, allowing for a wider reach and impact across diverse audiences. When you choose to be vulnerable and authentic in your storytelling, you invite others to reflect on their own journeys, encouraging them to recognize that they are not alone in their struggles and challenges. This realization—that these feelings are shared by many—can be incredibly powerful and validating, fostering a sense of shared humanity and connection that transcends individual experiences. Moreover, sharing your journey can serve as an empowering tool for others to confront their own imposter syndrome head-on and navigate through their insecurities. When individuals see someone they admire openly discussing their vulnerabilities along with the specific strategies they employed to persevere through tough times, it can ignite a spark of inspiration that motivates them to take meaningful and decisive action in their own lives. For example, if you detail how, you sought mentorship, engaged in deep self-reflection, or adopted a new, positive mindset that shifted your perspective, others may feel encouraged to implement similar techniques and practices in their own journeys, creating a ripple effect of empowerment that spreads far and wide. This ripple effect can cultivate a supportive environment where creatives feel emboldened to pursue their passions without the crippling fear of judgment or inadequacy. In turn, this fosters a thriving culture of resilience, growth, and collaboration, enabling everyone to flourish together while elevating the entire creative community as a whole. By sharing your journey, you not only contribute to your own healing but also play a vital role in uplifting others, creating a lasting legacy of strength and solidarity in the creative realm that echoes through generations. Additionally, creating spaces for meaningful dialogue can further amplify the impact of sharing your journey and enhance community connections. Hosting workshops, panel discussions, or online forums where individuals can freely and openly discuss their experiences cultivates a culture of support, understanding, and camaraderie among all participants. These spaces allow for the exchange of valuable ideas, techniques, and coping strategies that can benefit everyone involved and foster deeper relationships. By facilitating thoughtful discussions around imposter syndrome and the unique challenges faced in creative pursuits, you contribute to a collective healing process that helps dismantle the stigma associated with self-doubt. This paves the way for more open and honest conversations that can help individuals feel more at ease with their experiences, ultimately transforming their perspectives and reinforcing the importance of vulnerability in creative expression and interpersonal connections. Ultimately, sharing your journey can transform not only your own relationship with imposter syndrome but also significantly impact the experiences of those around you in profound ways. By illuminating the path, you have taken and the essential lessons learned along the way, you instill hope, resilience, and a profound sense of community in others. This reinforces the idea that overcoming self-doubt is a shared experience that many can relate to deeply and meaningfully, connecting individuals across various backgrounds and experiences. As you inspire others to embrace their own narratives and vulnerabilities, you contribute to a broader movement of authenticity and courage within the creative community. This collective effort paves the way for future generations of artists to thrive without the burdens of imposter syndrome, encouraging a lasting legacy of creativity that celebrates both success and struggle, weaving together all facets of the human experience in a beautiful tapestry. Ultimately, this fosters a richer, more inclusive artistic landscape where all voices and experiences are valued and heard, creating a vibrant tapestry of creative expression that can inspire countless individuals to pursue their passions wholeheartedly while feeling empowered to be their true selves and express their unique stories.

Don't miss out!

Visit the website below and you can sign up to receive emails whenever Stephen G. publishes a new book. There's no charge and no obligation.

https://books2read.com/r/B-A-VPPMC-FDIBF